A Study Guide to Help You

Grow Strong in Today's World

Donald Zoller

2

Grow Strong in Today's World
Copyright © 2022 by Donald Zoller

Cover Design by Liliana Zoller
Cover Image from Adobe Stock.
Used by permission.

Printed in the United States of America

A Dedication

This book is dedicated to you, my brothers and sisters in Christ. Particularly those of you who are in the struggle of life and death in Ukraine, both now and for months to come. May your lives demonstrate what being faithful to Jesus truly means to the rest of us. And, may you emerge from battle as bright lights in a dark world. May your wounds and scars radiant the glory and presence of God to bring healing and hope to your people—and to the world! *Thank you!*

Even though the fig trees have no blossoms,
and there are no grapes on the vines;
even though the olive crop fails,
and the fields lie empty and barren;
even though the flocks die in the fields,
and the cattle barns are empty,
Yet I will rejoice in the LORD!
I will be joyful in the God of my salvation!
The Sovereign LORD is my strength!
He makes me as surefooted as a deer,
able to tread upon the heights.

(Habakkuk 3:17–19 New Living Translation–NLT)

In Jesus' Name, Shalom!

Open My Eyes
A Prayer

Open my eyes, O Lord, that I may see
Chariots of fire,
And crowds of watching angels and saints,
The four living creatures of creation,
The hosts of the redeemed,
From every nation and every generation,
And You, standing in the place of power,
Directing your Kingdom and strengthening
Every struggling follower.

So seeing You, may I be held
Quiet and unafraid,
Ready and daring to be and do and bear all
That your loving wisdom allows or wills,
O beloved Author and Finisher of my faith.

George Appleton,
Missionary to Burma, 1902-1993

What's Inside ———

Table of Contents

Appendix:

*"Finally, be strong in the Lord
and in the Strength of His Might. "
Ephesians 6:10*

About the Author
By Connie Moyes
Teacher and Special Friend

I first met Don and Bev Zoller one Sunday morning in 2004 at Colonial Presbyterian Church in Kansas City, Missouri. They had just moved from Pinehurst, North Carolina, and were looking for a new church home. My husband and I facilitated an adult Sunday School class, and we needed help—we needed a teacher! Don was a Bible teacher and writer in North Carolina. (Among his publications are: *Learning to Suffer God's Way—Discovering Purpose in Suffering* and *The Last Shofar! What the Fall Feasts of The Lord Are Telling the Church*, which he co-authored.) Aware of how God answers prayer, I wasted no time seeking Don's help, and quickly he and Bev became members of our church—and Don was soon teaching our class.

As I listened and taught with Don, I learned he is a humble Bible scholar. His research is in-depth, and details are exact; he teaches with authority and sound judgment. In addition, Don has a great sense of humor and immediately connects with any group he leads. All these qualities make him a much-sought-after teacher. As a result, our class developed a deeper understanding of Biblical concepts and how to apply Biblical principles in everyday life. God's Word sets Don's moral compass, making him an excellent example for all of us.

Don's varied life experiences are many, which he shares on the pages of *The Master Weaver,* a recently published book. In the book, we discover his wonderful marriage of 56 years to his godly bride, Bev. We see how together they raised and nurtured three sons and cared for Bev's mother, Jean, during the last 25 years of her life.

His lifelong passion for maps led him to spend time in the Army Corps of Engineers and later to a 35-year career for the U.S. Geological Survey as a cartographer. His heart for missions took him on several international trips, caring for the spiritual and physical needs of the homeless, and working with a media ministry in the Middle East.

In later years, as he witnessed the progression of Bev's dementia, he learned how to be her caregiver, and finally suffered the loss after her death. All these, and so much more, have shaped the man Don is today. The results show up in his writing and teaching. He loves God and uses his gifts of teaching and writing to help others understand and navigate their path through this present-day world filled with cultural potholes and satanic attacks.

You will discover that *Grow Strong in Today's World* answers the following questions:
- What words would describe the world you live in today?
- What occupies most of your waking thoughts?
- Do you have feelings of dread, anxiety, or panic if you leave your cell phones at home?
- What does the phrase "my truth" mean?
- Why does God allow terrible things to happen in our world?

As you read this book, please be honest with yourself. Assess your truthfulness, what you hold in high esteem, and your relationship with God. Many of your answers may surprise you. Nevertheless, I hope you use this book to help you navigate a changing and challenging world by using God's Word as your "map."

The fear of the Lord is the beginning of wisdom, and the knowledge of the Holy One is understanding.
Proverbs 9:10

Before We Start

Why this Book Was Written

Without a doubt, we live in uncertain and challenging times. People from all walks of life are anxious and even *angry* about the direction of our society. Bitter divisions in our Nation's social and political fabric, increased violence, and ever-present injustices seem overwhelming. Such turmoil does not contribute to personal hope or domestic peace as enshrined in our Constitution and leaves great uncertainty about the future of our country.

Grow Strong in Today's World is more than informing *followers of Jesus* about the current state of our society. Instead, this book heralds a call to action to be alert, strong in faith, and to engage our culture with the Truth about God—His Word. Further, it is a call to be discerning about the present threat of our adversary, Satan. And to recognize the tools he masterfully uses to create turmoil among people—deception, despair, destruction, and death. Since the beginning of time, his tools have remained the same.

The book seeks to awaken followers of Jesus from a life of mediocrity to their God-empowered calling. It is a passionate calling to be bearers of His image, truth, and light in a dark and fallen world that desperately needs to know God. Further, it is an urgent call to advance the difficult work of His Kingdom. Time is short! Finally, the book pushes us toward intimacy with an awesome Sovereign God as a powerful, loving, and inseparable part of our lives—to be strong in faith in Jesus and His Word.

What's in the Book

The book has eight chapters and an appendix. We begin in **Chapter 1** by looking realistically at our world—*It's A Wonderful World–Not So Much!* Then, in **Chapter 2**, we examine *Idolatry— Both Then and Now.* Here we explore how idolatry of all shapes and sizes has consumed humanity, yes, even us, his Church. In **Chapter 3**, *What Is Truth?* we engage the agonizing subject that is millennia old but still under current debate. The question continues to create as much confusion as ever. **Chapter 4** directs our attention God-ward as we consider *The Sovereignty of God.* Here we ponder an incredible view of an unfathomable God. We will see what His sovereignty means to us practically as we engage our world.

Chapter 5, *A Republic—If You Can Keep It,* surveys the beginnings of our country, where we are today, and then confronts us with the provocative question, "Will it survive?" The question is followed by a challenge: What does our current National condition mean for us as followers of Jesus? Beyond our Nation, we want to hear *What God Says About Our World—And You.* **Chapter 6** covers this subject.

To become strong, we are now ready to exercise. **Chapter 7** lists *Eleven Exercises to Grow Strong.* Finally, in **Chapter 8,** we have our *Conclusion—So What?* We reflect on the issues covered in this book. Our challenge is to think and pray about what growing strong in faith means for us in today's world. Then to act! The *Appendix* includes a few items of interest that provides added information to our understanding of subjects covered in this book.

How to Use the Book

The book is a resource to be used as an adult Sunday School discussion curriculum, home group study, or individual study. There are plenty of opportunities to record notes along with your reading. You will find open space between paragraphs to write short thoughts. *"Your Thoughts"* at the end of each subsection within the chapter will give you additional space for notes. *"Additional Notes"* provide space between some chapters for more lengthy comments.

After each chapter is a list of discussion questions, *"Let's Talk About It."* From these questions, the group leader or facilitator and the group can select from the list of questions to be discussed as time permits. *Everyone* using the study guide needs to read the respective chapter and the Bible verses in bold font before the group meets. *Indeed, reading the chapter is a requirement for the leader or the facilitator.*

Final Thoughts

To *Grow Strong in Today's World* is not a Sunday afternoon easy-read. You will be required to think, interact, and, if needed, challenge what you read. Every effort is made to assure textual and biblical accuracy. However, you are free to investigate other sources to determine or reexamine your understanding. A yellow highlighter is recommended to mark the text for emphasis and reference. The objective is to personalize what you read.

Be sure to read all Scripture references in the bold-faced font. Reading the Scripture allows the Spirit of God to speak to you and provides His commentary to the text. Examining each verse will take time and thought. As you reflect on the verses, you will better understand how they apply to the text. Don't be in a hurry! *Pray and ponder!* (A helpful hint: Using a Bible app on your cell phone will give you more time to *pray and ponder.*) The Berean believers took what they heard and examined the Scriptures to determine if what they heard was true **(Acts 17:11)**. The Bible is your plumb line for Truth. *Be sure you use it!*

Names and labels change over time, sometimes quickly. As a result, the meanings attached to these identifiers also change. It is no longer enough to call ourselves "Christians" or even "Evangelicals." These terms may suffice for use within our walls (among fellow believers). However, our culture has given different meanings to these terms—meanings that do not adequately describe who we are, or worse, create associations that do not represent our true identity as belonging to Christ the

King and His Kingdom. Therefore, throughout the book, the term, *followers of Jesus* is used in most places instead of Christians, evangelicals, or believers. *Followers of Jesus* is a term that best describes to whom we belong and what we do.

Additional Notes:

Lord, may I so walk with You today
That when You speak
You need only to whisper.

To the choirmaster: according to Lilies. A Maskil of the Sons of Korah; a love song.

My heart overflows with a pleasing theme;

I address my verses to the king;

my tongue is like the pen of a ready scribe.

Psalm 45:1

Chapter 1

What a Wonderful World Not So Much!

The year was 1967. During the summer of that year, one-hundred and fifty-nine (159) race riots exploded across the Nation. It was called the *Summer of Rage*. Newark and Detroit riots were among the most violent—43 deaths, several hundred injured, 7,000 arrested, and over 2,000 buildings burned and looted in Detroit alone. Entire neighborhoods were destroyed.[1] Protests against the Vietnam War erupted worldwide. Communist China exploded its first hydrogen bomb and a Six-day War raged in the Middle East involving Egypt, Syria, and Israel. In addition, people were facing an uncertain economy with the possibility of a recession on the horizon (1969). These and more filled the canvas of events for that year.

It was also the year that Louis Armstrong released his popular song, *What a Wonderful World*.[2] The lyrics were definitely unrelated to the conditions in our country in 1967. Despair, loss, and fear were everywhere. But in a time of terrible turmoil, Louis and his songwriter tried to put a happy face on our world. They believed there was hope for a better future, that nature and friendship pointed the way. Although the song inspired a positive note, the happy face that Louis wanted never really stuck. With the assassination of Martin Luther King Jr., the following year and the Kent State University massacre in 1970, it was a sad and challenging time for the Nation.

Race riots are part of our national DNA. Our Nation never entirely solved the central issue of the Civil War. We need only to look at Chicago in 1919, Tulsa in 1921, Harlem in 1935 and 1943, Watts in 1965, San Francisco in 1966 (a riot that required two thousand National Guard with tanks to help local and state police quell the violence), and the Summer of Rage in 1967. With the assassination of Martin Luther King Jr. in 1968, many riots ignited across the country. All these, to name a few tragic moments in our history.

In fact, since the beginning of our country, there have been over 100 significant race riots, with over 95 occurring since the Civil War.[3] Although some recent improvements between races are noteworthy, the fundamental problems continue unchanged to this day. Chapter 5 discusses how the followers of Jesus relate to the issues of racial inequality and injustice.

Well, here we are—some distance in time from 1967. Today, some may still want to sing *What a Wonderful World.* But for many who live in this world—*Not so much! Action Against Hunger* reports that globally 811 million people go for entire days without eating due to lack of money, access to food, or other disruptions.[4] In addition, a 2019 *United Nations* report shows about 100 million people are homeless, and over 1.6 billion people lack adequate housing. Current social and political turmoil, global conflicts, and the effects of a changing climate only escalate these numbers.

These real-life human problems represent over 20 percent of the world's population.[5] Economists believe these negative statistics impacting global social and political order will only worsen over the coming years. The availability of adequate food and fuel sources in poorer nations will mean more homeless and hungry people, many of whom will die of starvation.

Further, the *World Health Organization* reports about 970 million people worldwide currently suffer from chronic mental disorders.[6] These are in addition to the countless many who regularly suffer from ill-health and disability. Drug addiction in 2021 in the United States saw the death of over 100,000 people, according to the Center for Disease Control (CDC). Further, over a million people died in our country from the COVID pandemic of 2020–2022, with many more suffering the irreplaceable loss of their loved ones. *What a Wonderful World—Not so Much!*

From that tragic moment in the Garden of Eden until today, sin and its consequences have devastated humanity. As we saw above, sin and its effects are well documented in past and recent history. Nothing about our fallen nature has changed since the Garden experience. Even though today we have more electronic "toys," the human condition remains an unrepairable tragedy **(Romans 3:23)**.

When God set out to create this world, He was pleased with the results and said, *"It was good."* How long that lasted, we don't know, but what we do know is that something He created made a mess of what was perfect. Now, *it is not so good!*

The cataclysmic event, in that perfectly divinely planted Garden, between two people, a serpent and a piece of fruit, set the stage for misery and death for all of us. Sin has effectively scarred all human relationships. Relationships between individuals, within families, among communities, and between nations—all are affected. More seriously, sin fatally fractured humanity's relationship with its Sovereign Creator with terrible and frightening consequences. In fact, everything God made—His creation—was severely damaged by man's rebellion and sin against his Creator **(Jeremiah 12:4; Romans 8:20-23)**.

The biblical record underscores the problem. Yet today, we continue to reap the fruit of sin. Although people try to avoid and deny the sin question, it is prolific. In the world broadly, and in our Nation specifically, those with eyes to see, know that sin is the fundamental problem. Sin causes human suffering, disease, corruption, violence, and death.

Your Thoughts:

The Watchman on the Wall

In **Ezekiel 33:1–9**, God told the prophet to select a man from among the people to be a watchman. The watchman, stationed on the city wall, warned the people behind the wall of impending danger by blowing his trumpet loudly so all could hear. Hearing the trumpet's blast, the people immediately protected themselves from imminent danger.

Today, God still provides a watchman to warn His people of impending dangers from a sin-infested culture. But, like the prophet of old, the watchman sees what few others see or care to see. In the days of Noah, what the watchman saw was not much different from what he sees today—suffering, corruption, and violence **(Genesis 6:11–13)**. *Today, the only difference seems to be how quickly the results of sin travel throughout our world.*

But, sadly, most pay little attention to the watchman's warnings. For them, life continues as it has been, and they ignore the coming danger. Others are fearful, angry, anxious, and uncertain about the future but lack understanding of what to do. In times of despair, they have no strength to resist the coming threat and are unaware of what has already breached the wall. As a result, they often shrink back and ignore the present danger **(Jeremiah 6:17)**.

What follows are eight observations about today's culture that can become problems for the followers of Jesus. The watchman warns you to be careful and *glue* yourself to God's Word as these problems seek to overwhelm you by invading your thoughts and behavior. Thoughtfully consider each one to see where today's culture seeks control of your life. These observations are in no particular order:

(1) Elections, local and national, can be a cultural intrusion into your life. Elections have a way of diverting your attention and energy away from God's Kingdom and forcing you to be focused on another kingdom—the kingdom of this world. Opinions and passions run high in a nation that is currently so socially and politically divided. The coming elections will be significant. Some state governments have already restructured their voting laws to ensure integrity and security and, as some believe, preemptively skewed results to assure a specific partisan outcome. They also believe if these elections are not as expected, violence and chaos are possible. Democracy, as it has in the past, will be challenged. Whatever the outcome of the elections, the watchman calls you, as a follower of Jesus, not to be a part of what divides this country. Instead, be alert and aware of election outcomes, stay focused on Christ, and be ready to communicate His *Shalom* (peace in conflict) in chaotic times **(John 14:27)**.

(2) Your culture is deeply narcissistic—self-centered, self-absorbed, and indulgent. It is highly susceptible to believe lies— little ones and big ones. Today, many people are rushing to the dark side of the internet and social media to form their worldview of "truth" based solely on misinformation, fabrications, and conspiracies. Deceived, they are victims of educated ignorance. They freely function in an alternate reality, an echo chamber of similar sounding voices. The watchman issues this warning to you

as a follower of Jesus, "Be careful!" You cannot drink from this polluted fountain of self-focus and delusion without serious results **(Thessalonians 2:11–12; 2 Timothy 4:3–4; Philippians 4:8)**.

(3) *"In a democracy, people deserve the government they have" (from a Constitutional lawyer).* In a democracy, we are the ones who choose our politicians. In some measure, those we vote for reflect what is in our own hearts. Unfortunately, the watchman sees many self-serving politicians who know or care little about our Constitution. They appear more focused on their reelection than governing for the benefit of the people. Consider the oath of office they recite before being formally seated in Congress:

I do solemnly swear that I will support and defend the Constitution of the United States against all enemies, foreign and domestic; that I will bear true faith and allegiance to the same; that I will take this obligation freely, with no mental reservation or purpose of evasion, and that I will well and faithfully discharge the duties of the office on which I am about to enter. So help me, God.

Regrettably, this oath is not a *daily* reading for those in Congress. It is said only once at the beginning of their term of office and, for most, is soon forgotten. Based on this oath of office, political leadership primarily measures a person's character, followed by quality of performance. Unfortunately, many politicians have forgotten this virtue.

Forgotten, too, is the process of governing honorably. To govern honorably means negotiating political differences to achieve a compromise that leads to a beneficial outcome—*for the people.* Instead, Congress' current behavior of hyper-political partisanship only contributes to social division and strife. *Sadly, honorable public service is another forgotten virtue for many.* If you are called upon to serve your country as a follower of Jesus, you need to demonstrate honorable service. Do not forget those you serve, as others obviously do. Furthermore, the watchman reminds you that you are, above all else, a servant of the King of kings and Lord of lords **(Romans 13:1–7; 1 Peter 2: 13–17)**.

(4) As the watchman scans our culture, he sees people frequently attacking each other verbally and physically. Social media often energizes overheated cultural wars, revenge politics, and other hot-button issues. Through computer-driven algorithms, social media only heightens harmful and violent misbehavior. Frequently, these behaviors explode in what would typically be non-threatening venues—school board meetings, airplanes, retail stores, even hospitals. These are symptoms of a more profound problem. At its core is the loss of mutual respect and failure to listen to one another. Simply, people have learned to distrust and hate one another. As the watchman weeps over a culture filled with strife and violence, remove yourself from what causes division. Be part of the solution, not the problem. Here is the warning from Jesus: **(Mark 3:25)**.

(5) The culture is in decline. Among many causes, one indicator of decline is the coarseness of speech. Profanity frequently laces casual speech at all levels of society. Men and women use profanity in the media, in the public marketplace, and among friends. Children, echoing the language of their parents, equally use such profanity. Coarse and defective speech is pervasive. Its everyday use betrays an absence of thoughtful and intelligent vocabulary, expressing a debased and flawed character. As a follower of Jesus, you must guard against using profanity in making your point. Apart from being wrong, it denies the One who should be in control of your tongue **(Isaiah 6:5; Ephesians 5:4; James 1:20; 3:5–12; 5:12).**

(6) Persecution of Christians is also increasing, specifically for Bible-believing followers of Jesus. The more culture slides down into the pit of darkness, the more you need to understand the reality of your new life in Christ. The watchman reminds you: *You are in the world, but you do not belong to the world* **(John 15:19; 17:14)**. As you determine to walk closer to Jesus and commit more fully to His Word, you will be increasingly out of step with your culture—a misfit! So, don't be surprised if the world hates you. Jesus says to expect it. *Such hate is a badge of honor!* **(John 15:20; Philippians 1:29; I John 3:13)**

There is no reason to believe that you will avoid severe persecution. Throughout history, persecution has been the pattern for God's people. It's promised **(2 Timothy 3:12)**. Current cultural trends make persecution predictable. Since your ultimate allegiance is to the Kings of kings and Lord of lords, His Word, and His coming Kingdom, the world, in time, will tire of you, no matter how many good works you do. Here is the reality: **(John 15:18–21).**

Remember, your brothers and sisters in the Lord throughout the world today fully know what it means to be loyal to Jesus *alone*, even upon the pain of death. Over 360 million people worldwide are currently being persecuted for their Christian faith. (Open Doors WWL 2022) *Your loyalty to Jesus will be the point of testing in any persecution, now and in the future* **(Hebrews 11:36–38; Revelation 2:10)**.

(7) The watchman sees a culture where paganism continues to increase. As we will see in Chapter 2, paganism and its expression in the abundance of modern-day idols saturate our culture. A culture without Christ—where the glory of God is unknown—is a pagan culture. Paganism increases the more culture removes God from its thinking. The Watchman warns the follower of Jesus to flee idolatry and live before a pagan culture as a chosen race, a royal priesthood, a holy nation, and a people for God's own possession **(1 Peter 2:9–12; 1 John 5:20–21)**.

(8) Our culture suffers from *lifestyle* infirmities. Based on a recent Centers for Disease Control and Prevention (CDC) report, obesity is a major infirmity in our Nation afflicting over 70 million people. Although there may be legitimate medical reasons why some people are obese, many are obese because of overconsumption of food and insufficient physical exercise.

Over 50,000 people commit suicide annually, making it a leading cause of death in the United States. Again, as with obesity, suicide can be connected medically to a severe mental disorder. But many choose suicide when life becomes too stressful, when their lives no longer make sense, or there are no other apparent alternatives.

Thirty-three million people use illicit drugs, including 2 million people with opioid-use disorders. Beyond that, 15 million people have a chronic alcohol-use disorder. Illicit drugs and overindulgence of alcohol are lifestyle choices caused by the stress of life or simply for enjoyment.[7]

The state of society's lifestyle health seriously weakens the fiber and potential of our Nation. It is a prime factor in any nation's failure and ultimate fall. In Chapter 3, we see how even followers of Jesus can be enslaved to some of these entrapments when the Truth and power of God's Word in our lives are neglected **(1 Corinthians 6:19–20; James 3:2)**.

These are but a few of the most apparent problems the watchman sees troubling our Nation. These problems seek to consume the followers of Jesus, and some of these have already afflicted the people of God. With time, other problems may surface that are even more demanding and alarming. So pay attention to God's watchman, listen to his warnings, and determine to be a *faithful* follower of Jesus.

Your Thoughts:

What You Should Never Forget

*We know that we are from God, and the whole world lies in
the power of the evil one. 1 John 5:19*

There are **two** things you should rehearse *daily* in your minds
and hearts if you are to grow strong in today's world:

__We know we are from God__. Knowing to whom *you belong*
and *where you come from* is critical as you relate to your world.
Being from God *(out of God we are, Gk.)* identifies your divine
origin, your new nature as to *who you are* in Christ, and your
mission to the world. Being *out of God, you are* His image-bearer,
His light-bearer, and His Truth-bearer to a dark, hopeless, and lost
world **(2 Corinthians 5:17–18)**.

Knowing you are from God also says a lot about where your
loyalties ultimately lie—to the Lord of all and His eternal Kingdom
(Luke 9:23–26).

__We know the whole world lies in the power of the Evil One__.
Since you know this, do not seek solutions to lasting peace,
happiness, and satisfaction from the world. No matter how noble
the intentions of governments or their institutions may be, they
cannot produce what uniquely belongs to Christ, the Prince of
Peace. He, *alone*, is your peace, joy, and satisfaction. *Be sure you
agree with that Truth.*

You must not invest your time and energy seeking power,
position, or influence in a world controlled by the Evil One. God
may call you to the spiritual battlefield of earthly power, position,

or influence, but it is for *His purpose.* Never forget to whom you belong *(Ref: Joseph, David, Daniel, Queen Esther, etc.).* Your time and energy belong to God alone **(1 Corinthians 7:23; Matthew 16:24–26).**

The world cannot be reformed. Neither can its behavior change politically or socially apart from prayer and repentance toward God. He *alone* can transform the human heart, the behavior of people, and the direction of our Nation.

That *the whole world lies in the power (control) of the Evil One* is a biblical fact that seems to be something many followers of Jesus forget or ignore. But you must be alert and awake to the deceits of the Devil. In some measure, evil contaminates every human aspiration apart from Christ, ultimately resulting in a nation against nation, a kingdom against kingdom. Many such activities are apparent, but others, however, are not. Concealed in the human heart, they are known only to God. As followers of Jesus, you are an alien and sojourner in this world. You live in a hostile land controlled by Satan. **(Ephesians 6:12; Matthew 4:8–9)**.

Remember, this world is passing away, nations come, and nations go. They disappear and are barely remembered, often, only as a footnote to history! But God remembers and will bring each one into account in the coming judgment. Punishment and destruction await this present world because of sin's universal effect upon God's character and His creation. **(I John 2:15–17; 2 Peter 3:1–7; Revelation 6:15–17).**

Your Thoughts:

I will never hear God's voice from His Word
Until I am convinced that God from His Word
Is speaking to me. Author Unknown

Let's Talk About It
(Group Discussion for Chapter 1)

1. **"What a Wonderful World" (Pages: 15–18)** How does this chapter title fit **Romans 3:23**? (Search Google for the lyrics to the song) One of the five tenets of the Reformation is **Total Depravity.** What is your understanding of this tenet? See: **(Mark 7:21–23; Romans 3:9–18; I Corinthians 2:14).**

2. **The Watchman on the Wall. (Pages:19–25)** The watchman sees eight **(8)** things from his perch on the wall. Which **one** is most concerning to you? **Why?** Are there others you wish to add? **Why?** Would you delete any observations from the list you think are not appropriate? **Why?**

3. **What You Should Never Forget. (Pages: 26–27)** Why should you not forget *(and always remember)* **I John 3:19**?

4. Are there other thoughts related to your reading you wish to discuss?

Additional Notes:

A traveler without knowledge is like a bird without wings.
2 Peter 3:18

Chapter 2

Idolatry
Both Then and Now

In this chapter, we will define and examine idolatry as it was in biblical times and as it exists today in our culture. We will see how idolatry prevents us, as followers of Jesus, from a closer walk with Him, weakens our witness to the world, and eventually addicts us to a lifestyle that does not honor our Lord. Finally, we will explore ways we can be free from idolatry's enslavement.

A Short History of Idolatry

God has a big problem with idolatry. Unending sin against God has assaulted His holy character from the very beginning. As we will see, idolatry in our culture has consumed our lives as a substitute for God.

Sadly, as God's image-bearers, we stubbornly bend toward substituting something or someone for Him. Idolatry starts as an issue of the heart when we determine God isn't quite enough. That unholy thought began with a tree in a garden. The fruit of the tree offered something to make us wise, knowing good and evil, and thus we could become like God. *For the moment, it tasted pretty good.*

However, God was not pleased! It took the death of an innocent animal to cover the sin of Adam and Eve. Banished from the garden, their life was sweat, toil, and trouble **(Job 5:6–7; 14:1)**. To this day, it remains the same. Such was the nature and extent of Adam's sin that it affected the entire universe, ultimately requiring a new earth and heavens **(Galatians 5:19–21; Job 15:15; 2 Peter 3:7,10,12–13)**.

The specific nature of the wickedness God saw in those pre-flood inhabitants is unknown. But whatever it was, it caused God to judge the world severely **(Genesis 6:5–7)**. It's a good guess that it had something to do with idolatry. Since idolatry originated in the thoughts of the heart, it produced a flow of evil and vile behavior that infected *almost* everyone and everything. And God was not pleased! *Things got very wet!* **(Genesis 6:17; Matthew 24:38–39)**

The next big idol that got everyone's attention was a tower—the Tower of Babel. This building project reached into the heavens—a tall, impressive tower. Such a tower is called a ziggurat upon which the people commonly built a temple to worship a god. However, its stated purpose was to "make a name for ourselves." Without God, its purpose was a monument to human achievement, a prominent gathering place for a prideful people—*"Just look how great we are!"* It was *idolatry!* **(Genesis 11:4)**

Here again, God was not pleased! Divine judgment was the result. The Lord dispersed the people of Babel throughout the world, the very thing they were seeking to avoid. Each group of people took with them their unique language and their distorted view of God, a view that made Him less than He is. From here, it all went downhill! **(Romans 1:21–23)**

Idolatry persistently scarred the history of the children of Israel. It began with a cow in the wilderness. Israel just left 400 years of Egyptian bondage and had witnessed the recent awesome miracles of Jehovah, their Deliverer. But they decided they needed more than God's miraculous acts and a fiery mountain. So, they made a cow, a golden one—something they learned in Egypt. It was the best they could come up with as a substitute for God. *A cow!*

But, you guessed it, God was not pleased! So, He sent them on a 40-year trek through a desolate wilderness until the first unbelieving generation that came out of Egypt died. However, learning nothing from their parents, the next generation followed a willful path of idolatry for many years. God spoke to Moses just before his death about how Israel would continue seeking after strange gods (idols) **(Deuteronomy 31:16)**.

Israel happily took the gods of their unbelieving neighbors and made them their own. Through the prophets, God made many unsuccessful attempts to woo them back to their Mt. Sinai covenant relationship. This "marriage" covenant clearly stated, *"You shall have no other gods before Me"* and that their love for God was to be for Him *alone*. But Israel had a different idea. In time, God, as promised, sent them into exile beyond Babylon **(Acts 7:39–43)**.

Even though Israel gave an outward appearance of worshiping God, their hearts were far from Him. They had a greater devotion to their many idols. Unashamed, they displayed them for all to see. Even in the Temple of God, idolatry was commonplace **(2 Chronicles 33:1–10; Ezekiel 8)**. Why would Israel do such a thing? Did they seek the acceptance of their idolatrous neighbors? Or, perhaps, was it to embellish their personal piety? Maybe it was to be inclusive of people with other forms of worship? But, most likely, as with the golden calf in the wilderness, it was an evil, sinful belief that God was not quite enough. *That He couldn't be trusted!* As they pursued their idolatry, in time, they forgot the God of their fathers **(2 Chronicles 24:18–19)**.

The broken heart of God fills the pages of the Old Testament. From the beginning, He told Israel not to make, worship, or bow down to idols **(Leviticus 19:4; 26:1–2 Deuteronomy 12:29–31)**. *He was all they needed.* But they paid no attention. Instead, with their pagan neighbors, they sacrificed their infant children alive in the fire on the altar of Moloch. There were over thirty such idols in Israel, many involving immoral sexual behavior[1] **(Ezekiel 23:37–39)**.

Here we need to pause for a moment to reflect. How is it with you? Like Israel, do the inclinations of your hearts take you away from your covenant of marriage with Christ? Do you find your "idols" more comforting, pleasurable, and fulfilling than your daily walk with Jesus? Nevertheless, the words of Mt Sinai still apply:

"You shall have no other gods before Me," and our love for God is to be for Him, alone **(Exodus 20:2–3; Deuteronomy 6:4–6)**.

When the Apostle Paul arrived in Athens, he saw a beautiful city of advanced culture, intellect, academic scholarship, and artistic beauty. However, these cultural amenities did not impress Paul. What impressed him was this—*the city was full of idols*. The worship of these idols tormented his spirit **(Acts 17:16)**. The city was over the top with the number and size of idols. Because many idols involved prostitution, the Apostle Paul made his point clear to the Church in **1 Corinthians 6:12–20**. As noted previously, idolatry is an issue of the heart, not the rationality of the mind. *You can be highly cultured and gifted with great intelligence, but still have idols in your life.*

Henry Martyn, an Anglican missionary, came to the city of Calcutta (Kolkata – renamed, 2001), India, in 1806. It was and still is the cultural center of Eastern India. In many respects, the city was like Athens. However, Calcutta had its share of idols exceeding those of ancient Athens. By the latest count, the number of Hindu idols is about 330 million.[2]

After Henry Martyn walked the streets of Calcutta, he returned to his apartment in the evening and broke down in tears of anguish. His deep sorrow was not because he could not share the Gospel, but like Paul, he saw the people consumed with their worship of many idols. They were not giving their worship to the true God as He rightly deserves. *Indeed, because of idol worship, God was robbed of His Glory.*

Your Thoughts:

_____

_____

_____

_____

_____

Why Is Idolatry So Bad?

Based on the brief history of idolatry from our previous section, there are four essential things we should keep in mind when thinking about why "my idolatry" is so bad.

1. **Idolatry** *(my idolatry)* disfigures and diminishes the image of God. It does not convey the truth of who God is nor defines His likeness. Instead, *it assaults the character of God:*

   *. . . and they exchanged the glory of the immortal God for images resembling mortal man and birds, and animals, and creeping things. (**Romans 1:21–23**)*

2. **Idolatry** *(my idolatry)* is a sign of blatant sinful rebellion and opposition to God's authority:

> *Far be it from us that we should rebel against the LORD and turn away this day from following the LORD by building an altar for burnt offering, grain offering, or sacrifice, other than the altar of the LORD our God that stands before His tabernacle!* **(Joshua 22:29)**

3. **Idolatry** *(my idolatry)* is demonic, for it embodies the essence of Satan. His purpose is to substitute and displace God by making Him irrelevant, thus robbing Him of His glory: *". . . I will make myself like the Most High"* **(Isaiah 14:13–14)**. Satan seeks our worship.

4. **Idolatry** *(my idolatry)* is sin and separates us from God. Anything can be an idol if it distracts you from the Lord as your *first love*. Even His blessings can become idols. He, and He alone, must always be the ultimate desire of your hearts.

> *You shall love the Lord your God with all your heart and with all your soul and with all your mind.* **(Matthew 22:37)**

Most people seek fulfillment in other people and earthly pleasures or achievements. Thus, they create idols before which they bow down. *"I will have no other gods before Me!"* Make God the deepest desire of your heart. Let Him satisfy your yearning for fulfillment.

Here is something to keep in mind: To bow down or give credence to an idol is beyond the limits of God's tolerance. He ultimately judges such behavior **(Revelation 9:20–21)**.

Remember, idolatry is a big deal to God! Satan is glorified, not God when an idol (god) is worshiped.

Throughout the world today, hundreds of millions of people physically and emotionally prostrate themselves by giving devotion and loyalty to idols—bowing to something or someone other than the immortal God. The shape, size, or kind of idol—a piece of wood or an electronic device—doesn't matter. Idolatry is an issue of the heart. For this reason, both the Apostles Paul and John tell us in no uncertain terms: *"flee idolatry (literally, run the other way!) and keep yourselves from idols"* **(I Corinthians 10:14; I John 5:21)**.

God is a jealous God. Being a jealous God is one of His attributes found in the Old Testament. The expression does not describe God as insecure but instead describes One who is highly protective of His Glory. Similarly, faithfulness protects marriage, and both parties jealously guard to protect it. In the same way, God is jealous of protecting His character. Idolatry must not diminish His Glory. Therefore, he will not share His Glory with anyone or anything – a piece of wood, stone, metal, or even mortal man as an object of adoration.

*. . . for you shall worship no other god, for the LORD, whose name is Jealous, is a jealous God. **(Exodus 34:14; Isaiah 46:9, 48–11)***

Be very careful to whom you attribute reverence and loyalty in your world today. There are many "false prophets," many in the guise of political or social leaders, who are seeking your loyalty—

*loyalty that belongs to God, alone. **(Matthew 7:15–20; 1 John 4:1)**.*

Your Thoughts:

_____

_____

_____

_____

How Idolatry Touches Our Lives

Yes, idolatry is still around today. Although our culture is sophisticated and technologically advanced, idolatry is still a big deal! It may not be as apparent as it was in Athens or Calcutta, yet it is pervasive. The followers of Jesus are not exempt! Many of our idols hide in our hearts. John Calvin, the great reformation preacher, said that *"the human heart is a perpetual factory of idols."*

Read what God says about *self-made* idols in **Isaiah 40:19–20; 44:9–20**. He describes a man that can't afford an idol. Nevertheless, this man spends a great deal of money, time, and effort making an idol from wood, only to burn part of it to cook his food and keep warm. Listen to how foolish God thinks this is:

The person who made the idol never stops to reflect, 'Why, it's just a block of wood! I burned half of it for heat and used it to bake my bread and roast my meat. How can the rest of it be a god? Should I bow down to worship a piece of wood?' The poor, deluded fool feeds on ashes. He trusts something that can't help him at all. Yet he cannot bring himself to ask, 'Is this idol that I'm holding in my hand a lie?' (Cited from the NLT)

The idols you cling to are just that, a lie. Deceived, you believe the lie your little idols can do for you what God cannot do. Remember His words to Israel and to you, *"I am all you need!"*

Today, we disguise most of our idols in our deluded hearts. But, remember, it's in the thoughts of the heart where we make our idols. As much as we try to hide them, God's eyes penetrate and know what is happening in our hearts. No matter how clever we think we are, we can't hide our idols from God. As a follower of Jesus, He has a particular interest in what goes on in our heart—*it belongs to Him.*

An idol is anything in your life that diminishes, substitutes, or competes for your affection and loyalty to God. Whatever consumes your desires, time, money, and energy *as a substitute for God* is an idol. You create an idol whenever you derive and seek your comfort, guidance, strength, and identity apart from God. **(Colossians 3:5–6)**. *Remember, idolatry in any form is always an insult to the character of God. **It is a sin!***

Let's be honest! Even as followers of Jesus, most of us struggle with at least one or two idols that hang around and have taken up residence in our lives **(James 3:2)**. We are not always aware of what they are, but there they are, on the shelves of our lives. Sometimes forgotten, but when needed, they are admired and embraced. From time to time, the Holy Spirit comes with His sword drawn (the Word of God) to clean house. How glad we are to be free of idols! However, it doesn't take long before we put them back on the shelf or find a replacement. Such is our inclination to create idols.

Commonly said: We are creatures of habit. We have good habits, and we have bad ones. Some of these habits can be addictive. They are so ingrained in our persona that we don't know we have them or can't seem to get rid of them. For most, it isn't easy to say, "Begone!" Some confess they just can't let go. They may excuse themselves and say, "I was just born this way." However, for the follower of Jesus, there is a way to be free of idolatry and *stay free.*

If we take seriously and prayerfully **1 Corinthians 10:13–14; 2 Corinthians 5:17**, we see God has provided a way. **The Way is Jesus**. Too often, when we think about these verses, we look within ourselves for the solution to get rid of bad habits, lifelong sins, and even our pet idols. We make resolutions we quickly break. We usually come up with some crazy ways of doing God's job. Too often, we forget Jesus, who, through His Spirit, is the only One who can purge the innermost places in our hearts—His Temple. He seeks to fill us with Himself—*without competition.* As God did with Dagon, the pagan god of the Philistines, He smashes stubborn idols that compete with His Presence. Ultimately, He *alone* can do it—in His time and in His way. And, since this is a spiritual battle with the Evil One, it requires persistent prayer and a faith that says, "Lord, only You can do it!" **(Mark 9:28–29)**

In our cluttered thinking, we forget who we *really* are in Christ. We are His children, clothed in His righteousness, and a new creation where old things have passed away. Behold, all has become new! *That's who we are!* Our constant challenge is to get from *where we are* to *who we are* **(Ephesians 4:20–24)**. As a refresher, go back to our key Scripture and ponder **I John 5:19**.

Your Thoughts:

What Are Some of Your Idols?

Let's take a hard look and examine some idols you may have in your life. Here are a few questions you can ask yourself to see what idols may lurk in your heart. Ask the Holy Spirit to illuminate and clean house in those darker, easily-overlooked places in your life. Try to be as candid as possible in your investigation. *Write down what your find!*

Where Do I Spend My Time?

Where Do I Spend My Money?

Where Do I Get My Joy?

What Occupies Most of My Thoughts?

Your answers may be long or short. But they will reveal where your idols are hiding. Unfortunately, these idols are engrained lifestyle behaviors that are not always easily removed.

These behaviors are your pet idols. But by resisting the Holy Spirit's warnings you erect a "No Trespassing" sign. Why? Because your pet idols bring you pleasure and emotional comfort. However, In seeking pleasure and comfort in such idols, you suppress the Truth of God's Word and grieve the Holy Spirit. You've created an idol that enslaves you to a life of bondage. Satan has you where he wants you **(1 Peter 5. 8–9)**.

At first, the bondage is subtle, even innocent in appearance, just like the fruit from the tree in the Garden of Eden. However, it soon becomes an entrapment from which escaping is exceedingly difficult. It is here that bondage to your pet idol can become an addiction.

Addictions occur when a person increasingly becomes dependent and obsessive about a thing or activity for comfort, pleasure, or fulfillment. Cravings, inability to stop, and lifestyle dysfunctions all point to some type of addiction—spiritual bondage and enslavement to an idol. *And, Satan is pleased!*

When you decide that God isn't enough when facing adverse life situations, you are vulnerable to an addiction—a severe form of idol worship. Adversities might include financial stress, destructive behavior, relationship pressures, family conflicts, and loss of purpose and direction. These lead to depression and addiction. Addiction becomes your idol and energizes your behavior. At this point, there is little room in your thoughts for God. Unfortunately, thoughts of God become an unwanted distraction to what you and your idol really want to do.

What follows is a list of addictions that *can* become your idols. If not correctly managed, you will find yourself obsessed and addicted by them. This will rob you of your affection and loyalty to God *alone.*

Although addictions can be physical or behavioral, the two are often closely related. These physical and behavioral addictions are listed in no particular order:

1. **Typical forms of physical addictions**—Frequent and obsessive use of:
   a. Alcohol
   b. Tobacco and other forms of inhalants
   c. Drugs, both illicit and prescription drugs.

   These physical addictions can devastate you, your family, and your friends. Therefore, the followers of Jesus must avoid the practice and even the attraction to these addictive idols.

2. **Compulsive Behavioral Addictions** are obsessions that can become your idols. They commonly include:

   a. Food Addiction.

   b. Social Media and Video Gaming Addiction

   c. Pornography and Other Sexual Addictions

   d. Social/Political Activism Addiction

   e. Cell Phone Addiction

   f. Work Addiction

   g. Exercise Addiction

   h. Astrology, including Spiritism Addiction

   i. Shopping Addiction

   j. Gambling Addiction

   k. Entertainment Addiction, including TV Binge-Watching, Video Gaming, Sporting Activities

   l. Personal Appearance Addiction

There are others, but you are encouraged to search Google for further information on these listed addictions.

For followers of Jesus, dependency on these and other physical or behavioral addictions is not only psychological but spiritual. Based on Pew and Barna research, several million evangelical Christians find themselves prisoners to many of these addictions.

If you are enslaved to any of these addictions, it is spiritual warfare, and you are not winning! Satan's ploy keeps you locked in bondage and from enjoying fellowship and intimacy with God, who took special care to create you!

Biblically, these addictions are idols to which many bow their knee, render devotion, and suppress the Truth. For the follower of Jesus to indulge in such addictions reflects a deficiency in the biblical knowledge of Truth and the power of our new life in Christ that has set us free from Satan's bondage.

So Jesus said to the Jews who had believed him, "If you abide in my word, you are truly my disciples, and you will know the truth, and the truth will set you free." **(John 8:31–32)**

Stay alert! Watch out for your great enemy, the devil. He prowls around like a roaring lion, looking for someone to devour. **(1 Peter 5:8 NLT)** *also,* **(Ephesians 5:10–18)**

Tamara Chamberlain, author and speaker, in her web posting, *7 Modern Day Idols that May be Creeping into Your Life* (https://herandhymn.com/2019/07/11/idols/) includes the following:

Be Careful What You Cling To

"Though there are many advancements in the times we live compared to bible times, we have not advanced past building up idols in our lives. We may think they are harmless or even justified. But Scripture is very clear about how God views idols.

"We can never be ignorant that each of us is prone to building an idol in our life—to invest, trust, and lean on that thing more than we do God. We must constantly tear down and burn up the altars of our idols to let God in. He wants to be the one to make us whole–not the many other things we cling to."

We can see why both the Apostles Paul and John warn followers of Jesus to flee from idols. So many times, the New

Testament warns us of being seduced by the things of this world to where they become the most important thing in our life, by definition, idolatry.

Listen to God's Word on the subject:

Do not love the world or the things in the world. If anyone loves the world, the love of the Father is not in him. For all that is in the world—the desires of the flesh and the desires of the eyes and pride of life—is not from the Father, but is from the world. And the world is passing away along with its desires, but whoever does the will of God abides forever. **(1 John 2:15–17)**

Then Jesus told his disciples, "If anyone would come after me, let him deny himself and take up his cross and follow me. For whoever would save his life will lose it, but whoever loses his life for my sake will find it. **(Matthew 16:24–25)**

Simply, idol worship is about divided loyalties. You cannot split your loyalties. Is your loyalty to Jesus and His Kingdom, or is it to the kingdom of this world? Or, as a preacher recently said, *"Do you follow the crowd or do you follow the Cross?"* You face this choice daily. To which will you be loyal? It can't be both. *It doesn't work that way.*

The Westminster Shorter Catechism of 1846–47 includes this profound statement: *"The chief end of man is to glorify God and to enjoy Him forever."* You cannot enjoy God when you do not glorify Him. And you cannot glorify Him when you are bowing down to the idols of your hearts. Do not be those who rob God of His Glory—I can think of no greater sin!

"I am the Lord; that is my name; my glory I give to no other, nor my praise to carved idols." (Isaiah 42:8)

48

Your Thoughts:

The God who changes not,
Continually interrupts our lives with change,
And most always we are upset by it.

Let's Talk About It
(Group Discussion for Chapter 2)

1. **A Short History of Idolatry. (Pages 31–35)** A phrase is repeated, *"God was not pleased."* Why was God not pleased? Why does God hate idols? (Hint: It is more than disobedience to God's command.)

2. **Why Is Idolatry So Bad? (Pages 36–39)** In **Romans 1:21–23; Isaiah 14:13–14,** What concerns God most in the practice of idolatry? How can your idolatry rob God of His Glory?

3. **How Idolatry Touches Our Lives. (Pages 39–42)** Why does God refer to idols hidden in your hearts as a **lie** that you hold in your hands? **(Isaiah 44:9–20)**

4. **What Are Some of Your Idols? (Pages 42–46)** Give a personal example of how an idol interfered with your relationship with God. What did you do about it? What difference did it make? What other idols might be identified besides those listed on **Page 48**? Why would you include them?

5. **Be Careful What You Cling To. (Pages 46–47)** What is the message from the quote on **Page 50**? What are your personal challenges as you consider **1 John 2:15–17 and Matthew 16:24–26?**

Additional Notes:

Too often the ways of God upon my life are relegated
To a place of convenience
Rather than to a place of dominance.

Chapter 3

What is Truth?

It was early morning. A noisy crowd had gathered in front of Herod's palace. The people were angry. They had gathered to confront Pilate, the Roman governor, about Jesus. Inside the palace, Pilate was questioning Jesus about the charges the religious rulers of Israel had made against Him. Calmly Jesus answered, *"I have come into the world—to bear witness of the truth. Everyone who is of the truth listens to my voice"* **(John 18:37).** Pilate's response was simple yet profound—a deeply perplexing question that still echoes through the corridors of human history, *"What is truth?"*

Philosophers and religious leaders still ask today the same question without a satisfactory answer. They spend much time parsing truth but arrive only with propositional theories about truth.[1]

Pilate eventually returned with Jesus to the riotous crowd. He asked what he should do with this One who bears witness to the Truth. Stirred on by their religious leaders, the cry of the mob echoes to this day, "Take Him away! Crucify him!" **(John 19:15)**

Thus, Truth was crucified. Many years before, Isaiah the prophet lamented:

Our courts oppose the righteous, and justice is nowhere to be found. Truth stumbles in the streets, and honesty has been outlawed. Yes, truth is gone, and anyone who renounces evil is attacked. The LORD looked and was displeased to find there was no justice. **(Isaiah 59:14-15 NLT)**

From the tree in the Garden of Eden to the present, assaults on the truth have been persistent. Today, many people frequently choose to believe a lie rather than accept the truth. The lie, whatever it is, becomes an idol to which people bow and sacrifice their integrity and deface the character of God. Telling a lie is a spiritual issue with moral consequences. Unfortunately, people are hopelessly bent toward believing a lie.

John Calvin understood the kinship between a lie and idolatry. He said that idolatry occurs every time the Truth about God is exchanged for a lie. If a lie is believed to be true, then an idol is created—an idol to which people will give allegiance and worship to the detriment of themselves and others.

We will let the philosophers and religious leaders pursue their quest to understand truth. Biblically speaking, the quest is a fool's errand. Instead, in this chapter, we will focus on what the God of Truth has to say about truth, where truth is in our world today, and how lies about the truth affect the followers of Jesus.

The Essence of Truth

The essence of Truth is God. That is who God is—Truth. Whenever anyone speaks the truth, they align themselves with God's character. Broadly defined, truth is an agreement with fact or the state of reality. What is "up" cannot be "down!" What is "right" cannot be "left." "Two apples plus two apples will always equal four apples," and so on. When using such logic, Truth is absolute.

Because God is Truth, He speaks Truth. The Scripture tells us, *"The sum of your word is truth, and every one of your righteous rules endures forever"* **(Psalm 119:160}**; and *"Your word is truth"* **(John 17:17)**. These statements declare absolute and objective truth about the Word of God. Only when sinful people question the authority of God's Word and reject the inspiration of Scripture does absolute truth become subjective, relative, and debatable. In rejecting Scripture, they repeat the infectious words of Satan, the father of lies, *"Did God actually say . . . "* **(Genesis 3:1)**.

Some may remember a radio program called *Truth or Consequences* or another game show called *To Tell the Truth*. These game shows ran for many years, beginning in the 1940s. More than anything else, they showed how people then thought about *telling the truth*. There were no "alternate realities," "relative truths," "subjective truths," or *"My truth."* Truth was just truth! It was absolute. A sincere handshake or a person's truthful word often concluded a business transaction. But not today! "In writing, please—with a signature"—is the expected requirement.

Our culture has severely diminished these former expressions of truth and integrity. We no longer trust one another to be truthful.

Today, people speak of truth as having many shades of meaning. Truth has become relative and subjective, determined by the situation or an individual's perception. Opinions become truth in these tortuous manipulations. Each of us can have our own truth. It may not be your truth, but that's okay. "I have *my truth*," which is just as valid as your truth, even though it may be unashamedly false. Isn't that nice—we can both sleep peacefully tonight!

This false understanding and constant acceptance of opinions as truth lead to cultural and moral decay. Not so long ago, words and actions that were inappropriate, unacceptable, and sinful are today accepted as a matter of individual choice. Lying, cheating, stealing, immoral sexual behavior, and even ending life in the womb have become irrelevant in the personal behaviors of many. Suppressing the Truth eventually corrupts the entire Nation.

In our present world, people have a bag full of scrambled and personalized opinions, and *all* equally true—so convenient in a time where "up" is "down" and "right" is "left" and where two plus two can equal anything we might want. The American Worldview Inventory of 2021 shows that 54% of Americans (180 million people) embrace the postmodern idea that all truth is subjective and there are no moral absolutes. Unfortunately, many of our younger politicians are among that number. As Isaiah said many years ago, *"Yes, truth is gone, and anyone who renounces evil is attacked" (Isaiah 59:15 NLT).*

A tree in a field may help understand the popular idea of truth. Here is the fact: A tree is growing in a field. Some say the tree is too large and should be cut down, or too small and be moved to another location. Others may wish to deliberate, negotiate, and even vote on what should be done with the tree. But the issue is still about an *existing* tree. However, based on the American Worldview Inventory, many would say *the tree doesn't exist.* They conclude there is no tree in a field. For them, *this is an alternate reality.*

Like Adam and Eve, people often hide from the Truth. They say, *"I was they misunderstood." "I was a victim of fake news." "That's not what I meant!"* or *"What I said was taken out of context."* Pointing their accusing finger at others, they readily blame others for their lie. Yet, *in most cases,* in simple language, *"They are lying!"* They lie without conscience before a watching world and commonly *lie without consequences.* Often, our culture gives them a pass with a shrug of the shoulders, thus, perpetuating the lie.

Most people don't seem to be offended when others tell a lie. Telling a lie has lost its sting. Even in many respected places in society, lying is almost a non-issue. But there are still exceptions to this "Alice in Wonderland" world. In testimony before Congress or in our courts, to lie is a felony. Yet, some still try to avoid telling the truth, denying the oath just taken before the court and God. *For them, truth means nothing.*

If we care about the truth, we must be vigilant in speaking truth to our culture—a culture where truth can mean anything that expediency requires. Yet, followers of Jesus know the one true

God, the power of His Word, and that Truth is absolute. We are responsible for being God's Truth-bearers in our post-modern world where *truth stumbles in the streets, and honesty has been outlawed.*

Telling the truth in all situations can be challenging. Truth can hurt and be difficult to communicate. For example, how would you answer a terminally ill family member or friend when questioned, "Am I going to die?" Yet, if done with love, wisdom, and awareness of the situation, telling the truth is needed. Truth seeks its time to be said **(John 13:6–7)**.

You may remember the story of the old Italian woodcarver named Geppetto. He carved from wood a boy named Pinocchio. Geppetto told his creation that he would become a *real* boy if he proved himself brave, *truthful*, and unselfish. Unfortunately, as with so many of us, Pinocchio had a problem with the truth. What happened? His nose grew longer and longer each time he told a lie. I wonder how many people need to look in the mirror and check the length of their noses?

On a personal note: I had my first encounter with truth when I was about five years old. I told a lie to my mother. When you tell a lie to your mother, it's like telling a lie to God. You can't get away with it. Immediately, I underwent a procedure that reinforced the value of telling the truth. My mother washed my mouth out with soap! Today, we might refer to that remedial action as child abuse, but it made the point. The value of telling the truth, *not an alternate reality,* was indelibly etched on my mind and is so to this day. God bless my mother—a teacher of truth!

Your Thoughts:

_____

_____

_____

_____

Where Did the Lie Begin?

Lying, not telling the truth, has a clear origin. The Bible tells us exactly where lying began. Like most everything else that speaks to our fallen human condition, not telling the truth began in the Garden of Eden. God spoke the Truth about a particular tree. _"If you eat it, you will surely die."_ But Satan, the father of lies, said. _"You will not surely die."_ Think about that. Satan was accusing God of lying and that he, the Serpent, was the truth-teller. Essentially, saying, _"You can't trust God to tell you the truth— you can't trust His Word."_

That's a lie that keeps on giving! It has permeated all of human experience and, in subtle ways, it even creeps into our lives as followers of Jesus. Remember, when we cannot trust God for what is right, we express doubt about His goodness. To doubt is to disbelieve. To disbelieve is to say *God's Word can't be trusted. Do we then say God is a liar? This gets serious in a hurry! **(Titus 1:1–3; Hebrews 6:17–19;)***

I imagine the garden conversation went something like this: *"Adam. You know that tree of the knowledge of good and evil? You know, the one God said not to eat its fruit? Here, have a bite! The serpent said it was okay. He said God really didn't mean what He said."* Today, the serpent still says, "The Bible? That's not what it *really* means!" The implication is profound!

People, by nature, choose what is most convenient, even if that choice is wrong. They prefer to believe and *promote* a lie rather than tell the truth, particularly when telling the truth is inconvenient. Truth becomes a sacrifice upon the altar of expediency, pragmatism, and self-affirming convictions. Often, lying promotes and protects our self-interest—ME! Yet, we still look for *a place to hide behind.* Whenever God speaks, He speaks the Truth, *revealing who we are and the lie we are hiding within our hearts.*

Jesus said, "I am the way, *the truth,* and the life." Truth is fundamental to the character and nature of God. To lie is one of those things God can't do. Therefore, as followers of Jesus, truth is not a disposable commodity. Here's the warning: *We are His Truth-bearers, and we had better get it right!* As bearers of His Truth-we constantly must shine the light of His Truth into the dark places of our culture.

The darkness of our culture is heard and seen in the places we go for entertainment and information. These can include what we consume on television, our social-media devices, the movies we see, or anything else that twists the truth like a pretzel into a lie.

Remember, the essence of truth is all about the character of God. Anything that does not bear the stamp of truth diminishes His character. In a truth-deprived world, we are to reflect who He is to the lost. Our lives will reflect the presence of Christ when we live daily *Coram Deo (before the face of God)*, immersed in God's Word and prayer. We then are ready to speak the Truth about God regardless of our circumstance or opposition—anywhere where the glory of God is unknown **(Exodus 34:29; Matthew 5:15–16; 2 Corinthians 4:5–6)**.

Your Thoughts:

_____

_____

_____

_____

_____

_____

Listening to God About Truth

Let's take a time-out and listen to God as His Word speaks about Truth. He leaves no doubt about the source of ultimate Truth:

*Thomas said to him, "Lord, we do not know where you are going. How can we know the way?" Jesus said to him, "I am the Way, and **the Truth**, and the Life." **(John 14:56, Emphasis mine)***

Jesus not only bears testimony to the Truth **(John 18:37),** He is the incarnation of Truth. This makes searching for Truth wonderfully simple. It's found in a person—the person of Jesus Christ. All you need to do is bring all life questions to Him. Jesus is the answer. Answers can come from a text of Scripture, a life experience, or a word from another brother or sister in Christ. The answer may come from simply asking, *"What would Jesus do or say?"* Be patient! When the answer comes, you will know you have the Truth. Regardless, the answer comes by prayer, reading His Word, *and a still small voice* **(Isaiah 30:20–21)**.

*Teach me your way, O LORD, that I may walk in your truth; unite my heart to fear your name. (**Psalm 86:11**)*

God's Word also says the Truth sets you free *". . . and you will know the Truth, and the Truth will set you free" **(John 8:32)**.* A lie puts you into shackles—bondage to the lie. You are no longer free. Typically, one lie gives birth to another lie and another. You become a slave to the lie, with each lie being easier to tell than the previous lie. But God's Word assures you that you can be free and live your life in the Truth.

We are from God. Whoever knows God listens to us; whoever is not from God does not listen to us. By this we know the Spirit of Truth and the spirit of error. (1 John 4:6)

To reemphasize the point, Jesus says:

And I will ask the Father, and he will give you another Helper, to be with you forever, even the Spirit of Truth, whom the world cannot receive, because it neither sees him nor knows him. You know him, for he dwells with you and will be in you. (John 14:16–17)

But when Truth is ignored, God speaks loudly:

For the wrath of God is revealed from heaven against all ungodliness and unrighteousness of men, who by their unrighteousness suppress the truth (Romans 1:18).

You are of your father the devil, and your will is to do your father's desires. He was a murderer from the beginning, and does not stand in the Truth, because there is no truth in him. When he lies, he speaks out of his own character, for he is a liar and the father of lies. But because I tell the truth, you do not believe me. (John 8:44–45)

Lying lips are an abomination to the Lord, but those who act faithfully are his delight. (Proverbs 12:22; 2 Chronicles 18:4–27)

A warning: Lying to the Church (to other brothers and sisters in Christ) is an abomination to the Lord, and His judgment is swift! (Acts 5:1-11).

Your Thoughts:

Practical Thoughts About Truth

Be careful where you drink! Don't drink from a polluted fountain. *Neither should you seek truth from a world under the control of the Evil One. Instead, drink where the Truth is found—in Jesus (John 16:13–14).*

Many people anxiously seek truth through social media such as Facebook, Instagram, TikTok, or Twitter, and news channels, magazines, and other sources, where opinions often masquerade as truth. What they see and hear are words that may be untrue but told as if they were true. Remember, disinformation and opinionated "truth" intentionally captivate you by design. For example, watching a *single* news broadcast as your source of truth can produce similar self-affirming *echo-chamber* results. What is false—untrue, dishonest, and deceptive—all packaged as the truth pollutes your mind. Remember, only *the Spirit of Truth* can help you discern good from evil. *Ask Him!*

If anyone teaches a different doctrine and does not agree with the sound words of our Lord Jesus Christ and the teaching that accords with godliness, he is puffed up with conceit and understands nothing. He has an unhealthy craving for controversy and for quarrels about words, which produce envy, dissension, slander, evil suspicions, and constant friction among people who are depraved in mind and deprived of the truth . . . (I Timothy 6:3–5)

Be discerning! Keep truth pure, undiluted by opinion. Do not believe what is untrue, regardless of how many people believe and say it is true. A lie fundamentality remains a lie no matter how many times what is false is repeated as truth. Because so much in our culture is tainted with what is false, make a habit of going to the only source you can trust as true—the Word of God. Avoid jumping to conclusions on any subject. Instead, fall to your knees in prayer and ask *the Spirit of Truth* what you need to know **(Proverbs 4:20–27)**.

*If any of you lacks wisdom, let him ask God, who gives generously to all without reproach, and it will be given him. **(James 1:5)***

*. . . so that we may no longer be children, tossed to and fro by the waves and carried about by every wind of doctrine, by human cunning, by craftiness in deceitful schemes. **(Ephesians 4:14)***

The media is full of unavoidable noise. Therefore, it becomes difficult for people to know who or what to believe. People become cynical, trusting no one except what they hear in their own echo chamber. We live in a hyper-demanding society that requires knowing the facts NOW, and invariably those "facts" come up short of the truth. In frustration, people conclude with the Psalmist, *"All men are liars" **(Psalm 116:11)**.*

*For the time will come when people will not put up with sound doctrine. Instead, to suit their own desires, they will gather around them a great number of teachers to say what their itching ears want to hear. They will turn their ears away from the Truth and turn aside to myths. **(2 Timothy 4:3-4)***

During the final chapter of human history, the coming of the lawless one will take the Lie to a new level as he aligns himself with Satan. He will display great power through signs and wonders that serve to amplify the lie. His wickedness will be pervasive, deceiving those who are perishing. They perish because they refused to love the Truth and so be saved. For this reason, God sends them a powerful delusion so that they will believe the lie and be condemned because they have not believed the Truth, but have delighted in wickedness. **(2 Thessalonians 2:9-12)**

(Thank the Lord you are not like that!)

Your Thoughts:

_____

_____

_____

_____

_____

Living the Lie

Lifestyle choices abound in our culture. Our society encourages and provides a wide range of choices. However, for the followers of Jesus, your options are limited. Whatever your preferred lifestyle choice may be, it is always to be godly and in line with the Word of God. Rejecting or ignoring the Truth will leave your life exposed to the Lie—Satan's lie about God and you. This exposure quickly places you in dangerous territory. Soon, as a deceived victim of Satan's lie, you become enslaved and in bondage to him. You will be *living the Lie* **(1 John 1:6)**.

The Lie happens in the heart, unseen at first by most people. You think only you know the lie you are living. Therefore, you try to cover it up—*hiding it by deception.* You hide it from others and try to hide it from God. That is impossible with an all-knowing, all-seeing God. *It doesn't work!* **(Psalms 90:8)**

The lie you live consumes your thoughts, time, and energy. Even though you regularly attend church, God rarely occupies your thoughts or affections. Such lifestyle choices become addictions, and you have created an idol. Unfortunately, many people in our culture are addicted and entrapped by living a lie, including followers of Jesus **(Galatians 1:6; 1 Peter 5:8–9)**.

In Chapter 2, a list of some present-day idols is noted. Each one represents a lifestyle choice that can become the unholy lie you live. Unfortunately, you can live a lie without knowing you are in bondage and enslaved to Satan's purposes. He intends to make you the focus of your self-affirming attention, such that you trust in yourself and not in God. *That is idolatry and living a lie!*

To better understand how an idol can become the lie you live, the following are descriptive examples selected from the list of idols in Chapter 2. Background data and information for these descriptions are mainly from the Pew Foundation Research, Barna Research, and other research organizations listed in the End Notes of the Appendix. You are encouraged to do a Google search for further information about the following examples:

1. **Entertainment/Activities.** To be entertained or be involved in various activities bring enjoyment to life. But when entertainment or activities become a consumptive obsession—something that defines who you are and something you must have, you may be living a lie and thus, creating an idol. It may be TV binge-watching, live theater, sports, exercising, computer games, travel, or excessive time spent on social-media. Any one of these can quickly become a lifestyle addiction—an idol. Being busy for the sake of being busy can also lead you away from intimacy with God. But they all become lifestyle addiction disorders. If these activities are *priority one* in your life, God isn't! So much of idol worship today centers on trying to be entertained, happy, and fulfilled—all without God. *That's a lie!* **(Colossians 3:1–6)**

2. **Personal Appearance.** As God's people, how you appear to others is important. However, if outward appearance becomes more important than the attractiveness of the indwelling Christ, you have created an idol and are living a lie. Being obsessed with self-image, personal appearance, or occupied with what others think of you enslaves you to an idol. You are living a lie of bondage that is not a Christ-like lifestyle.

   Men and women both share this problem. This *lie* may include spending *excessive* time before our bathroom mirror, at the nail salon, at the gym, or even consuming the latest quick-fix diet book to enhance your self-image to make a good impression on others. As a result, you erroneously believe that your identity is on the line, forgetting that *Jesus is your identity*. Your self-image can become one of the most unsuspecting idols in your life. When your appearance becomes more important to you than how God sees you, you *have an idol problem* and are living the Lie **(I Peter 3:3–4)**.

3. **Family.** Our families are important. God makes it abundantly clear in His Word that we should love and care for them. They are important to Him, and they should be important to us. However, as people age, families can become a *consuming obsession—an idol*. This obsession is apparent when we feel compelled to be involved in every detail of our family's life—in every decision they make. The family becomes our singular focus and much of our time revolves around them. Because our compelling need is to be with our family we frequently excuse ourselves from doing what God wants. Loving God by caring for the needs of others receive what little time and energy are leftover. Our families have become our idol. And the life we are living becomes a lie **(Genesis 2:24; Matthew 16:24–25; John 21:15)**.

4. **Job/Career.** The Apostle Paul doesn't excuse laziness: *"If anyone is not willing to work, let him not eat"* **(2 Thessalonians 3:10)**. However, by contrast, your job or career can consume most of your time and energy. This often results in sacrificing family and church. If this is the case, you either have the wrong job, or *you have an idol and are living a lie.* If your goal is to achieve a rewarding career without God's direction, you are missing the mark.

Consider the words of Scripture: **(Matthew 16:26; 1 Timothy 6:6–10)**.

5. **Safety and Security.** Nowhere in Scripture are you promised safety and security in this world. Yet, you live in a culture that demands both. Media ads often tell you how unsafe and insecure you are if you don't have a house security system, a gun or guns, a generator in case of a power outage, and certainly virus ware to protect your home computers. If you follow your culture, you will be driven by fear and insecurity. *You have not surrendered your fear for safety and security to Jesus, who alone protects your life. He alone is your security!* When you are overly concerned for your safety and security, when these become a lifestyle addiction, you are in bondage to an idol and living a lie **(Psalm 56:3–4; Psalm 121:1–8; Matthew 10:28–31; Romans 8:38–39; 2 Timothy 4:18)**.

6. **Sex and Pornography.** Sex can be a blessing or a curse. God created and wonderfully designed it. It is a blessing you receive in marriage. Sex becomes a curse when abused. Our culture's general acceptance of promiscuity and unfaithfulness has wreaked havoc on marriages and families. Unfaithfulness touches even the lives of the followers of Jesus—both those in the pews and behind the pulpit.

Pornography is another form of sexual abuse. The viewing of pornography by men and women has increased with the use of the internet and other social media. Watching, fantasizing, and virtually engaging with pornographic content is a lifestyle choice. It is a compulsive obsession that touches and enslaves the lives of millions. And, like others, followers of Jesus are being seduced and addicted to this distorted view of sex.[2] *Simply, it is an idol, but a big one!* **(Matthew 5:27–30; I Corinthians 6:15–20)**

7. **Cell Phone Addiction.** Your cell phone is a blessing of present-day technology. Besides being a wonderfully convenient communication device, it is the most unique and comprehensive information tool in human history. The positive benefits of your cell phone are abundant but, unfortunately, the use of the cell phone is abused. Spending excessive time on your cell phone has become an idol for many. Cell phone addiction is the gateway to social media, text messaging, gaming, video watching, and chatting with like-minded friends about things that may be of questionable importance. Based on statistics, *eMarketer.com* has determined that most Americans spend almost 4 hours a day on their cell phones. With TV viewing, the total screen time is over 7 hours per day.[3] This excessive time is not only unhealthy emotionally and physically, but spiritually.[4] Many seek personal connection and identity approval through their cell phone. Here are a few of the symptoms to see if your cell phone has become your idol:

   a. Trouble completing tasks at work or home,

   b. Isolation from family and friends,

   c. Concealing your cell phone use,

   d. Having a "fear of missing out" (FOMO) when you're not on the phone,

    e. Feelings of dread, anxiety, or panic if you leave your cell phone at home, lose your battery charger, or worse yet, lose your phone.

It is difficult to see how one can have a meaningful relationship with God along with all the chatter and emotional stress that can come from your cell phone. **(Psalm 101:3)**

8. **Social/Political Activism.** Our society legally allows and often encourages you to participate in social and political causes at whatever level you choose, within the limits of the law. Participating may mean actively taking part in rallies, marches, public hearings, and administrative duties. All these are lawful in an open democracy. However, for the follower of Jesus, involvement in cause-oriented efforts will require spiritual discernment and, in some cases, may be questionable. At issue is a lifestyle choice that can become an addiction in pursuing a cause—albeit even a legitimate cause.

The problem is this: You can quickly become consumed and entangled by the demands of your chosen cause which leaves little room in your life for God's Kingdom. Remember, apart from repentance toward God, our sinful culture is unredeemable. Whether the cause is social justice or political activism (right or left), without the power of God's Word to transform lives, these efforts are ultimately unsustainable, unfruitful, and empty.

As the times and seasons appear to be approaching a climax for your culture and your world, following Jesus, and Jesus only, is the higher calling on your life. Following

Him, promoting the Gospel, and advancing the Kingdom of Heaven are activities that contribute to an eternal purpose and a permanent solution to current problems. Today's causes, and there are many, all clamor for your attention. However, to give your time, energy, and loyalty to any one of these causes is a lifestyle choice that can become a consumptive obsession, an idol, and a life of living the Lie **(1 Corinthian 6:12; 2 Timothy 2:3–4)**.

These are only a few ways that compulsive obsessions can become idols based on lifestyle choices. If there is any lifestyle addiction in your life, let it be the addictive passion and devotion to Jesus so that He may be glorified in everything. *"I press on toward the goal for the prize of the upward call of God in Christ Jesus" (Philippians 3:14)*

Your Thoughts:

Let's Talk About It
(Group Discussion for Chapter 3)

1. **The Essence of Truth. (Pages 53–56)** How would you describe the *essence of truth* to an unbeliever, and why should they care? What do **Psalm 119:160** and **John 17:17** say about Truth, and what does that mean? Describe the difference between objective and relative truth.

2. **Where Did the Lie Begin? (Pages 52–59)** What was Satan's lie, and what was the implication of that lie? What are some examples of how the lie shows itself in today's culture? How does the lie affect you?

3. **Listening to God About Truth. (Pagers 60–61)** Which Scripture verse was most impacting for you? Why?

4. **Practical Thoughts About Truth. (pages 62–64)** Look at **Proverbs 4:20–27**. What does the father tell his son about the changes in behavior truth can make? How do these words relate to your life? How does having the Spirit of Truth in your life make a difference in your decisions?

5. **Living the Lie. (Pages 64–71)** Describe how lifestyle choices become addictions? From the list of examples, which ones do you think are most common among followers of Jesus? Why? Have you ever had to hide your lie? What did you do about it?

Chapter 4

The Sovereignty of God

You are here today not by some biological act alone, but most significantly because God, as Sovereign, willed it so. His sovereignty touches the magnitude of a seemingly endless universe while completely controlling the very essence of who you are at your sub-atomic level.

Although we can never plumb the breadth and depth of God's sovereignty, in this chapter we will briefly explore how His sovereignty touches every dimension of His creation, including us. We will also see how His sovereignty undergirds our walk of faith with Christ and our witness to the world.

Come, Meet Your Sovereign God

The nation of Israel was in Egypt for over 400 years, much of that time in slavery. Being immersed in the worship of Egyptian gods, they forgot about the God of Abraham, Isaac, and Jacob. God called Moses not only to deliver His people from bondage but to re-introduce them to Himself. Thus, God directed Moses to write the first five books of the Old Testament—Genesis, Exodus, Leviticus, Numbers, and Deuteronomy. Moses taught and introduced Israel to God from these books, saying, "Here is your God, the God of your fathers."

Moses first met God in a burning bush in the desert near Horeb, the mountain of God **(Exodus 3:1–6)**. From this unexpected encounter, God spoke to Moses and declared His name "I AM WHO I AM"—*YAHVE! (Yahweh).* The root word is Arabic, meaning *love, desire, and passion.* Over the years, the "unsayable" name of Yahve was further developed by Jewish scholars who gave it a deeper understanding.[1] John Piper, a noted pastor and Bible teacher, gives us a brief account of the nature of Yahve, the name of God.

1. Yahve never had a beginning. Nobody made God. God simply is. And always was. Without beginning or ending **(Genesis 1:1; Psalm 41:13; John 1:1–3)**.

2. Yahve will never end. He did not come into being, nor can He go out of being because He always *is*. He is all that ever was, eternally. Before He created, there was no space, no universe, no emptiness. Only God. *Before the beginning of all things, God was! And continues to be, forever!* **(Psalm 90:2; Isaiah 57:15; Hebrews 13:8; Revelations 1:8)**

3. Yahve is utterly independent. He depends on nothing to bring Him into being or give Him support, counsel, or make Him what He is **(Isaiah 46:8-10)**.

4. Everything that *is*, depends totally on Yahve. The entire universe is utterly secondary and dependent on God for its existence. It came into being by God and remains moment to moment by God's decision to keep it in place. That includes people—you and me. The entire universe is nothing compared to God **(Psalm 24:1–2; Daniel 4:34–35; Revelation 4:11)**.

5. Yahve is constant. The essence of Yahve cannot be improved. He is who He is. He is not becoming anything. Without a shadow of change in the past, present, and future, He is the same yesterday, today, and forever **(Psalm 102:25–27; Ecclesiastes 3:14; Malachi 3:6; James 1:17)**.

6. Yahve is the absolute standard of truth, goodness, and beauty. There is no law book to which He looks to determine what is true. There is no judge or official He looks to for authenticating facts. He neither consults a museum or gallery to assess what is excellent or beautiful. He Himself is the essence of what is true, good, and beautiful **(Isaiah 40:13–15; John 17:17; Romans 11:33–35)**.

7. Yahve does whatever He pleases. He is always right and always acting consistently according to who He is. He is utterly free from any constraints that do not originate from the counsel of His own will (e.g., God can not lie.) **(Job 42–2; Psalm 135:6–7)**.

8. Yahve is uniquely the most important reality in the universe and eternity. Therefore, He is more worthy of our attention, adoration, and enjoyment than all other realities, including people and stuff that clutters our lives **(Philippians 2:9–11; Revelation 4:9–11)**.

Interestingly, Jesus attributes to Himself all that Moses found in Yahve. Jesus said to the religious leaders, *"Truly, truly, I say to you, before Abraham was, I am."* **(John 8:58)** In **Revelation 1:8**, the resurrected Christ reinforces that claim, **"***I am the Alpha and the Omega," says the Lord God, "who is and who was and who is to come, the Almighty"* **(See: Isaiah 9:6–7)**.

In summary, these descriptions of Yahve show how He is the absolute Sovereign in name, character, and being. He is the One who overflows in love, desire, and passion. He is the One who Moses met that day at the burning bush.

We, too, need to be re-introduced to our God. We need a burning bush moment. *It is for us to ponder deeply these attributes of Yahve's name.* Only then can we grow in our understanding of how awesome our God truly is; only then will we be able to handle the troubling times we are now living.

On a personal note: I have a book on my library shelf that has found a special place in my collection. It has been so for almost 40 years. It's one I return to many times for encouragement and spiritual enrichment. As a fictional story written by *Gene Edwards*, it is the most beautiful love story ever told. *The Divine Romance* stretches from eternity to eternity, wonderfully revealing the sovereignty of a loving God. He is the One filled with desire and passion, moving with a singular purpose to secure a Bride for Himself. As the story unfolds, we see how the eternal God in Christ, fiercely attacked by Satan, secures and glorifies His Bride. In most cases, I would be cautious about recommending a fictional story to convey Truth. Some may question the theological assertion that

God had a need outside Himself for companionship, i.e., the Bride of Christ. But, that apart, I feel this book is exceptional. Without a Table of Contents or Chapter Titles, at least in my edition, *The Divine Romance* is the stage the Holy Spirit uses to draw the reader from one playact to the next. Go to the End Notes and find out how you can add this unforgettable book to your library.[2]

Your Thoughts:

_____

_____

_____

_____

_____

_____

_____

_____

_____

_____

When it comes to the mighty movements of the Spirit, every heart is either a highway or a hindrance. Isaiah 40:3

How Big is God?

"In the beginning, God *(pl. Elohim)* created the heavens and the earth." **(Genesis 1:1)**

From the beginning of time, man has scanned the heavens. But for thousands of years, his observations were limited. He saw the arrangement of stars and named the celestial constellations. However, not content with God's purpose for creating the heavens to be an abiding witness to His awesome sovereignty, man devised an idol—astrology, an ancient religion universally popular even today in horoscopes and other practices.

About 400 years ago, the telescope was invented. This invention allowed the first peek at the mysterious vastness of the universe. Today, NASA's two powerful telescopes are probing the universe—the Hubble Telescope and the James Webb Space Telescope. What they see is only a tiny "nit" of the total breadth of the universe, which contains billions upon billions of galaxies with mega-trillions upon trillions of stars. A child once asked an astronomer, *"How many stars are there?"* His reply was simple yet profound, *"As many as there are grains of sand upon the beaches of the world"* A whole lot!

Lift up your eyes on high and see: who created these? He who brings out their host by number, calling them all by name; by the greatness of his might and because he is strong in power, not one is missing. (Isaiah 40:26)

He determines the number of the stars; he gives to all of them their names. Great is our Lord, and abundant in power; his understanding is beyond measure. (Psalm 147:4–5)

Within the counsel of the Trinity, God, in and through His Son, created everything. In the beginning, the Word that was made flesh already existed.

The Word was with God, and the Word was God. He existed in the beginning with God. God created everything through him, and it created nothing except through him. (John 1:1–3 NLT)

The Son is the image of the invisible God, the firstborn of all creation. For by him all things were created, in heaven and on earth, visible and invisible, whether thrones or dominions or rulers or authorities—all things were created through him and for him. And he is before all things, and in him all things hold together. **(Colossians 1:15-17)**

Some say that Jesus is the cosmic glue that holds everything together and keeps it from flying apart.[3] **(Colossians 1:17)**

The whole created order—the heavens and the earth—all belong to Him as Creator. It is all His! He owns it all! This profound thought gets close to where we live. Since it is all His, in truth, none of what we have is our own. As it was in the Garden of Eden, we are only stewards—custodians of God's abundant gifts to us. *"Nothing I possess in this life belongs to me!"* **(Psalm 24:1; Colossians 1:16)**

Understanding our role as curators of His gifts, we can live before Him with open hands to receive or release whatever pleases Him and brings Him the most glory. Here is the profound truth: Even our very life does not belong to us **(Job 1:20–22; I Corinthians 6:19–20).**

*The earth is the LORD 's, and everything in it. The world and all its people belong to him. **(Psalm 24:1 NLT)***

*Behold, to the LORD your God belong heaven and the heaven of heavens, the earth with all that is in it. **(Deuteronomy 10:14)***

*The heavens declare the glory of God, and the sky above proclaims his handiwork. Day to day pours out speech, and night to night reveals knowledge. There is no speech, nor are there words, whose voice is not heard. **(Psalm 19:1–2)***

From these verses, we can determine three things about God's sovereignty:

1. First, God in Christ *created* all things—everything!
2. All things, including people, *belong* to Him.
3. As Sovereign God, He *controls* all things. There is not one thing He doesn't control—from the most distant star to the smallest atomic particle. Therefore, nothing exists outside of His sovereign control.
   a. God controls the affairs of nations **(Job 12:23; Psalm 33:8–15; Isaiah 30:28)**.
   b. God controls the affairs of individuals—you and me **(Job 12:24–25; Proverbs 16:33; 19:21)**.

Why, then, are you so anxious about what goes on in your world? God is still in control. Do you really believe this?

*Peace I leave with you; my peace I give to you. Not as the world gives do I give to you. Let not your hearts be troubled, neither let them be afraid. **(John 14:27)***

The Sovereignty of God is all-encompassing, particularly at the personal level. He knows all about us—far more than we know about ourselves. Jesus reminds us that the very hairs on our head are numbered **(Matthew 10:30; See: Psalm 139:1–18)**. Though our finite minds may struggle with the idea, the Apostle Paul tells us that God, as sovereign, has mercy on whom He wants to have mercy, and He hardens the hearts of whom He wants to harden **(Romans 9:17–18)**. All our decisions ultimately comply with His sovereign will **(Proverbs 21:1–2; Acts 4: 27–28)**. Without question, He may do whatever He pleases without consulting with His creation—you or me **(Romans 11:33–36)**.

Yet, many within the Church today reject or minimize the idea that God is *totally* sovereign. This rejection happens when the thought of God's sovereignty interferes with what we think or want. God's sovereignty also interferes with our thinking when our sense of fairness conflicts with His sovereign justice. We want to remain in control of our lives. When we don't fully accept God's loving sovereignty over our lives, we are the losers. Such a rejection is idolatry. A.W. Pink, in his book, *The Sovereignty of God,* calls this *"the deification of the creature rather than the glorification of the Creator."*

Your Thoughts:

Practical Implications

Before moving on, let's refresh our minds with our key verse from **1 John 5:19**. *"We know we are from God, and the whole world lies in the power of the evil one."* Weaving this verse into the fabric of our lives is critical as we consider the practical implications of the Sovereignty of God.

Without disturbing the essence of the truth of this verse, you can easily insert, *"We know we are from the Sovereign God."* Just as Jesus was sent into this world, you are sent into your world bearing the exact imprint of God's sovereignty **(John 20:21)**. Consider how this imprint works out in your life:

1. **Because you are from God**, you have His *shalom*. *"Peace I leave with you; my peace I give to you. Not as the world gives do I give to you" (John 14:27)*. What the world gives is circumstantial and conditional peace. The peace that comes to you from Jesus is sovereign peace—His *shalom*. This peace is eternal and flourishes amid conflict and chaos.

    People around you are tied up in knots of anxiety, fear, confusion, anger, hate, and rage. Not peace, and indeed not the *shalom* that Jesus offers. *Be careful not to be overwhelmed by a world that has no peace!* Do not share in their anxieties. They know nothing of God's sovereign peace. Your ministry to your unbelieving neighbors is to quiet their fears with the calming words of Christ's love and His sovereign peace.

Don't forget, you are in this world but not a citizen of this world—you do not belong to it. You are from God, a citizen of heaven, and you are God's light, truth, and image-bearers in a world shrouded in darkness and fear. From God's Word, you already know how everything ends. You are on your way to heaven, and your destiny is to be face to face with Jesus. *Keep your focus!*

Don't despair! The Book of Revelation is for your comfort and encouragement. It comes to you with God's blessing **(Revelation 1:3)**. Although it speaks of future events, the big picture of Revelation is God's sovereignty—*Jesus wins!* That Jesus wins is a biblical worldview to embrace to be strong in faith and to have an effective witness to your time-bound world.

If you do not embrace this view, you will soon find yourself in the same fretful quicksand as the rest of the world, crying out for help. Jesus is our *shalom*! As you deal with today's problems, always keep what's up ahead in view. *Jesus wins!*

2. **Because God is Sovereign**, He removes from you all worry. Nevertheless, as followers of Jesus, you can fall into a pit of anxiety. You become anxious and spend a lot of energy fretting over what you cannot control. When you worry, you need to ask, "What is it about the Sovereignty of God I don't understand or believe?" He is in control of every situation, every circumstance. You may hide behind the word "concerned." To be concerned and not worry is a slippery

slope to navigate. It is all too easy to find yourself sliding into the pit of worry.

When you worry, the awareness of Christ's presence in your life is blocked. Worry is a major culprit in keeping you from growing strong in your faith. Many tend to accept worry as an inescapable fact of life. However, worry is a form of unbelief. Therefore, it grieves the Holy Spirit that is in you when you worry. *If you believe you are in charge of your life, then certainly you do have cause to worry.* But since God is sovereignly in control of your life worry is both unnecessary and counterproductive. Remaining confident in God's sovereignty is His cure for your anxiety. Trust the One who unconditionally loves you no matter what lands on your doorstep.

*Do not be anxious about anything, but in everything by prayer and supplication with thanksgiving let your requests be made known to God. **(Philippians 4:6)***

3. **Because God is Sovereign**, fear is unnecessary. Along with worry, fear seeks to destroy you. When your stress level goes up, your physical health goes down. Fear will always cloud a beautiful relationship with Jesus. Whatever the circumstance, even when the world crumbles around you, there is no need to be afraid! With great passion, Jesus frequently tells those He loves, *"Do not fear!"*

Fear wraps its tentacles around your mind and heart when you doubt and do not believe God is able to deal with your problem—that God isn't enough! Your fear may come when you feel insecure or from personal events such as job loss, money concerns, a child's health or yours, or other hardships. Likewise, fear can come when world events seem uncertain or threatening. But that's not who you are in Christ. *"For God gave us a spirit not of fear but of power and love and self-control" (2 Timothy 1:7).*

> *God is our refuge and strength, a very present help in trouble. Therefore, we will not fear though the earth gives way, though the mountains be moved into the heart of the sea, though its waters roar and foam, though the mountains tremble at its swelling. Selah (Psalm 46:1–3)*
>
> *Even though the fig trees have no blossoms, and there are no grapes on the vines; even though the olive crop fails, and the fields lie empty and barren; even though the flocks die in the fields, and the cattle barns are empty, yet I will rejoice in the LORD! I will be joyful in the God of my salvation! The Sovereign LORD is my strength! He makes me as surefooted as a deer, able to tread upon the heights. (Habakkuk 3:17–19 NLT, Underline is mine.)*
>
> *There is no fear in love, but perfect love casts out fear. For fear has to do with punishment, and whoever fears has not been perfected in love. We love because he first loved us. (1 John 4:18–19; Isaiah 41:10)*

4. **Because God is Sovereign**, you can trust Him to complete His sanctifying work in you. Moreover, your salvation, and all that follows, has been God's sovereign plan and purpose for you before the foundation of the world **(Ephesians 1:3–10)**. Therefore, instead of focusing on your failures or striving toward self-improvement, focus on getting to know Him more intimately.

How foolish can you be? After starting your new lives in the Spirit, why are you now trying to become perfect by your own human efforts? **(Galatians 3:3 NLT)**

And I am certain that God, who began the good work within you, will continue His work until it is finally finished in the day when Christ Jesus returns **(Philippians 1:6 NLT).**

5. **Because God is Sovereign**, He gives you your sense of true identity. When you understand how exceedingly powerful your Sovereign God is and how much he loves you now and for eternity, you can be confident and completely secure in that knowledge. When you allow Him to define who you are as a new creation in Christ, you understand that He alone gives you your worth and your identity in Him. You have no further need to look at the changing ideas of this world to figure out who you are. *Neither do you need to keep chasing the never-ending fads of your culture.*

When you understand that your sovereign God controls absolutely everything, you are free to live and enjoy a wonderful-loving relationship with a truly awesome God. There is no need to fear or worry about failure or the final destruction of this world **(Romans 8:1)**. And you no longer need to fret about being worthless. You are a child of the King, the Sovereign Lord. That's who you are *now*, not in the sweet by and by. *You are from God!* That is your identity—*now and forever!* **(1 John 3:2–3)**

Your Thoughts:

_____

_____

_____

Submitting

Your sinful nature does not submit easily to the Sovereignty of God. You resist, make excuses, and even say, "No!" By nature, you dislike giving up control of your life. Submission goes against everything your culture teaches you about how to respond to the trials of life. Your culture tells you: "Be self-sufficient! Take charge of your life! Be confident about your ability to control life's changing situations!" This is what you know how to do best! But is that what God wants you to do? Listen to Jesus as He prayed to His Father, _"Nevertheless, not as I will, but as You will"_ **(Matthew 26:39)**.

Submitting to the Sovereignty of God is difficult. It takes time and practice to stop worrying and being afraid. Surrendering to His sovereign purpose for your life is difficult because you still want to have your hand on the throttle, controlling your life. To submit appears frightening and even dangerous, but it is absolutely the safest place to be. Surrendering becomes more effortless and almost irresistible once you taste and experience His loving sovereignty. So don't be anxious or fearful. Instead, immerse yourself fully in Christ's *shalom*. **(Psalm 34:8–10)**.

Experiencing the Sovereignty of God is a matter of the heart and the mind. It is a new way of seeing and interacting with your world. Knowing that God is *totally* sovereign is essential to your witness before a watching world. Remember, He who is sovereign *over all things* will help give meaning and purpose to your witness as you navigate the culture of this world. This understanding will provide a new perspective for your witness as you speak to those where His glory is unknown and who know nothing of God's love in Christ,

But here is a warning: Whatever part of your life is not submitted to God's sovereignty *contradicts* who you are. When you resist, excuse, or say "No!" to His sovereign presence, you diminish your witness to the world and severely impact your relationship with Him. *An unsubmitted life to the Sovereignty of God is never a good thing!*

Your Thoughts:

Let's Talk About It
(Group Discussion for Chapter 4)

1. **Come, Meet Your Sovereign God. (Pages 73–77)** Eight characteristics for *Yahve* described the name of God. Which ones were the most meaningful to you? Why? In your *own words*, how would you describe God to someone?

2. **How Big is God? (Pages 78–81)** How does the "bigness" of God affect your thinking about your life? Give specific examples of how you can let the world overwhelm you **(page 89)**. Do you have an issue about God being *totally* Sovereign in your life? What are those concerns? Why?

3. **Practical Implications. (Pages 82–86)** Why do you *worry, fear, and feel insecure* since God is sovereign? Jesus frequently told His followers not to fear. Why? **(Read Matthew 6:25–34)** How has knowing God is sovereign changed your thinking and behavior?

4. **Submitting. (Pages 87–88)** Why is submitting to God's Sovereignty over your life a problem? Specifically, what are the submission-problem areas in your life? Why? (if you care to share)

5. Do you have other thoughts you wish to share?

Additional Notes:

Faith is not a distant view, but a warm embrace of Christ
—John Calvin

Chapter 5

A Republic
If you Can Keep It

Like most summer days in Philadelphia, the weather was hot and humid. On this mid-September day of 1787, Mrs. Powel and a few other women of like-minded interest in politics waited patiently outside Independence Hall.

Inside, delegates from the former thirteen English colonies had been meeting since May. On the 17th of September, they completed a Constitution for the people of this new Nation. Their many sessions were long, intense, and heated. Through the morass of conflicting opinions, they debated, *prayed*, argued, and *prayed* some more. Finally, they arrived at a compromise. With a finished Constitution in hand, it took another year for the States to ratify the document. It took another three years before its Amendments, The Bill of Rights, were ratified in December 1791.

But on this day, the delegates' last meeting was over and soon, they emerged from Independence Hall. When Benjamin Franklin came out, Mrs. Powel wasted no time asking him, *"Well, Doctor, what have we got, a republic or a monarchy?"* Without hesitating, Franklin responded, *"A republic, if you can keep it."* His statement is haunting. It begs the question: *After 235 years, how well are we keeping our Republic?*

From the Federalist Papers of this period, the *Founding Fathers* viewed this new Republic as an *Experiment.* The Framers were less than confident that this Republic would make it.

A republic is a *concept* where the ultimate political authority is vested in the citizens of their nation. The character of a republic form of government depends on its citizens' civic virtues. A constitution or similar document usually enshrines these virtues. But the Framers rightly questioned if its citizens' civic virtues would preserve the Republic from corruption and moral decay. In many ways, our Nation was founded after a previous republic—*the Republic of Ancient Rome.*

Your Thoughts:

_____

_____

_____

_____

_____

_____

Our Roman Connection

When discussing our Republic, we begin where the idea of a republic began. We start with Rome. As we do, we also need to see how Rome lost their Republic and became autocratic, an Empire—*a rule by one man.*

The idea of a republic reaches back about 2500 years to what today is Italy. Rome was not always an empire ruled by Caesars. Before the empire, there was a republic—a republic form of government that lasted over 500 years. Before becoming a republic, the northern Etruscan Kingdom ruled Rome for almost 300 years. Brutal and oppressive, this kingdom took from the Romans the wealth of their lands and laid heavy taxes on them. But in 509 BC, the Romans revolted, defeating the Etruscan king and his army. Rome was free—free at last! *As much as we were at the end of our Revolutionary War.*

The Romans, like us, having won their freedom, moved forward to create a government that would never again give ruling authority and power to *one person*. But, they also knew that the pure democracy of the Greeks wouldn't do. So, they created a republic. Like the American Republic 2500 years later, Rome had a bicameral legislative system, with a constitution in which elected officials shared power among the Patricians and Plebeians. But, initially, these elected officials could only serve one year.

Rome had three classes of people – the *Patricians,* who were the elites—the wealthy and influential landowners; the *Plebeians,* who were the majority—the working class, merchants, farmers, and craft workers; and *the slaves,* who made up about a third of the population. These enslaved people were property with no rights, much like it was in our country for so many years.

This new Republic experienced many bumps along the way, with infightings, external wars, and social strife. Toward the end of its 500-year life, the Republic had become burdensome—so many laws and regulations. The rich were getting richer, and the poor were getting poorer. The lack of public interest and involvement in civic duties, disagreement over immigration, and issues regarding citizenship were long-standing problems. Divisions within the Senate and among the people became extreme. Nothing got done. The wealthy made sure they kept themselves in power. Corruption prevailed while the economy experienced an uncertain future. Many believed the Republic was in its death throes.

Then entered Julius Caesar. As a charismatic leader, Julius proposed a better way forward. He rallied support from the working class, the Plebeians, for an authoritarian form of government. Many were eager to have something better than the current Republic. They wanted a government that was strong, stable, and fair. However, this new approach was too much for the wealthy Patricians who supported a republic. Desperate to protect their way of life and power, the Patricians arranged for Julius to be assassinated.[1]

However, removing the threat only exacerbated the conflict between those who supported the Republic and those who did not. A civil war ensued. Over 200,000 men met on the Plain of Drama near Philippi in 42 BC to settle once and for all the destiny of Rome: Will Rome continue to be a Republic, or will it become an Imperial State? Finally, in 27 BC, the Republic lost the war. An imperial form of government replaced the Republic under Caesar Augustus, Julius' son. Power and authority were *once again* centered *in one person*. Caesar Augustus gave the Senate what they wanted—wealth and job security. They became his rubber stamp. As they say, the rest is history.

Clearly, there is a message for us. Where are we today in the life of our Republic?

Your Thoughts:

A mission field is all a matter of where you are standing.

Forming a Democracy

Early in this Nation's formation, John Adams, one of the Founding Fathers, gave his *prophetic* observation. He saw how our Republic would emerge to become a democratic institution where the people, its citizens, would govern themselves:

"We shall very soon have parties formed; a court and country, and those parties will have names given them. One party in the house of representatives will support the president and his measures and ministers; the other will oppose them. A similar party will be in the senate; these parties will study with all their arts, perhaps with intrigue, perhaps with corruption, at every election to increase their own friends and diminish their opposers." (John Adams, July 1789)

A few years later, John Adams made this statement:

"Our Constitution was made only for a moral and religious people. It is wholly inadequate to the government of any other." (John Adams, October 11, 1798)

As the people began to rule this Republic, Samuel Adams, a cousin to John Adams, critiqued this emerging democracy:

"A democracy never lasts long. It soon wastes, exhausts, and murders itself. There never was a democracy that did not commit suicide." (Samuel Adams)

In the minds of our Founding Fathers, the success of our Republic was very dubious. *"If you can keep it!"*

America was formed as a republic, not a democracy. This may surprise some. One of the easiest ways to understand what a republic is, is to understand a pure democracy.

Democracy, in its purest form, is simply a majority rule. If 51 percent of the people want something, then they get it. Most people will say, "Yes, that's what we want, majority rule." (That's what the ancient Greeks had briefly) But wait a minute. What if the majority decides they want your house? What if the majority decides they'd like to have your children? You'd say wait a minute; there's something wrong with that! Yes, there is! And you might strongly say you can't do that. I have my rights, and *the Constitution of the United States protects them.* And those protected *rights* define the nature of a *republic*.

Because of what is going on in our country today, many are concerned about the future of our Republic and its Constitution, *and we should be!* But, of note, the Constitution makes no mention of *political parties.* Instead, the focus is on the Republic, as is our Pledge of Allegiance:

I pledge allegiance to the flag of the United States of America and to the republic for which it stands, one nation under God, indivisible, with liberty and justice for all.

(Francis Bellamy,1892) Last revised,1954

As an American, your *allegiance* is to *the Republic* of the United States of America and its Constitution, not to a political party, regardless of which one you support. If the Republic dies, and with it the Constitution, *political parties will not matter.* They will be a non-issue. So, never fall on your sword for a particular political party! Never take up a cause that elevates a political party above the needs of the Republic. And, never allow a political party to define your country.

In today's world, extreme partisan loyalties have caused division and hate. Our Nation is a *Republic* for which our flag is the symbol! Political parties may drape and embrace the flag of the United States, but the flag and what it represents is *never* about a political party. It is about the Republic! Political parties have no ownership of the flag. Instead, the flag represents a *union* of separate states with powers derived from its people. That union shares in common with its people the rights enshrined in the Bill of Rights of the Amendments to the Constitution of the United States of America.

Climb up another rung higher on the ladder and see our country as our Founding Fathers saw it, *One Nation Indivisible—a Republic!* And, with that, *Liberty and Justice for All.* But, with added importance, we adhere to it as *ONE NATION Under God.* Here, there is no place for partisan politics!

Remember, the nature of political parties divides the Nation into "us" and "them" groups of opinionated and often intractable positions. The concept of a Republic unifies the Nation around a common Constitution, Flag, National Anthem, Pledge of Allegiance, and a common understanding of what "We the People" collectively means in practice—a shared and functioning democracy. These are the essentials of our Republic, the expression of which we together celebrate as patriotism.

Therefore, while political parties come and go, the Republic needs to be preserved at all cost. *Unfortunately, we as a Nation rarely behave as a unified Republic.*

During these chaotic political times in our country, where deep divisions and hate are pervasive, our focus, indeed our passion as American citizens, is to preserve our Republic *at all cost*. Don't forget the words of Benjamin Franklin: *"If you can keep it."* But, unfortunately, there is no guarantee that we can or will. *Remember Rome!*

Your Thoughts:

_____

_____

_____

_____

_____

_____

God commanded, but there are difficulties.
That's paralysis!
There difficulties, but God commanded.
That's power!

Our Country and God's Kingdom

We will now look at how we, as followers of Jesus, relate to our country and to the Kingdom of Heaven. First, we need to appreciate what will be said is unique to nations where the people rule within democratic forms of governments. In autocratic forms of government, followers of Jesus will behave differently. They have a different role, often living under extreme conditions. Our brothers and sisters in the Lord may not enjoy the freedoms we have in our country and may be the objects of persecution and extermination. Usually, there is much suffering. However, no matter where God places us in this world, for whatever purpose, and in whatever conditions we face, we all share the same biblical mandate found in **Mark 12:17; Romans 13:1–7; 1 Peter 2:13–21; 1Timonthy 2:1–4.**

As citizens of the United States and followers of Jesus, i.e., citizens of Heaven, we carry the burden of two citizenships. A burden because there is an issue of loyalty. Such divided loyalty or allegiance can cause tension. In this section, we will attempt to clarify that tension.

While we need to be concerned with the durability of our Republic, we who are followers of Jesus Christ need to keep in view the Kingdom of God as *our highest priority*. By so doing, we will effectively pray and seek the welfare of our Republic **(Jeremiah 29:7)**.

Salt and Light

As followers of Jesus and His Kingdom, we are to be *salt and light* in the place God has put us. *(In this free land by Thee our lot is cast—hymn, God of Our Fathers)* As salt, we are *to preserve* and *bring healing.* To preserve, we are to pursue what is good, true, and right—honesty, respect, truth, family values, and whatever else biblically contributes to the welfare of our Nation.

As salt, we also bring healing to our land. Among the many ways to do this, one way, as agents of God's love, is to dispel hatred toward those who are the outcasts and the most vulnerable of our society. Jesus makes clear what knowing Him means in our relationship to victims of social disparities—the poor and marginalized. As His followers, we are to give help and hope to the "least of these." It doesn't matter if the vulnerable, marginalized, and victims of injustice speak or behave differently from most of us **(Luke 10:25–37; John 3:16).** *We are not called to be agents of hatred and division, but agents of hope and shalom.* As image-bearers of God we are to make Him known to all people, even to the *"least of these"* **(Proverbs 31:9; Matthew 25:31–46).**

Daily Jesus made friends with sinners. His critics accused Him of spending time with sinners, prostitutes, and drunks. We sometimes forget that when Jesus said *God so loved the world*, God's love includes *all people*—the outcasts and the low casts. *There is no more compelling force in all the universe than the love of Christ to transform an individual or to change a culture.* Touching the heart, not its politics, is the way to seek the welfare of our Republic. It is the way to bring healing to a hurting Nation and ensure that God's will is *"done on earth as it is in heaven."* Be generous dispensers of *Christ's love and His Shalom*!

As Light, you are here *to expose* spiritual darkness, injustice, and corruption and *to illuminate* the path forward. As God's light-bearers, you must speak truth to power without hesitation in whatever form that may take. Your example is John the Baptist. He spoke truth-to-power in the face of death **(Matthew 14:1–12).** It could come to that! Be sure that God has placed and arranged His words for you to speak before you open your mouth. Exposing spiritual darkness is hard, but sometimes necessary.

Christ, the hope of glory, is the Light that illuminates the path forward—the light He has placed in our lives. When so much around us speak of darkness and hopelessness, our lives are to reflect the light of Christ's presence in love, mercy, and peace. In tangible ways, we are to show others the encouragement and hope that is ours. By our lives and words, we are to show there is another way to navigate through the darkness of injustices and afflictions of this life toward a certain future—a future with Christ in Heaven.

As salt and light, we are to influence and infuse our culture, not through political or social activism, but by building Christ-directed relationships with people all around us—touching the lives of the hopeless and helpless with the love of Jesus.

If our thoughts and energies are focused on our Father's Kingdom and His love for *all* people in our Republic and beyond, we will have no time to be entangled in civilian pursuits **(2 Timothy 2:3–4).**

Brothers and Sisters, that's who we are! **Salt and Light!** *That's what Jesus requires us to be!* **(Matthew 5:13–16)**

Your Thoughts:

Our Role and Our Nation

Because we live in this land we call the United States of America, our biblical role and responsibility are to pray for our Republic—*(all)* those in leadership **(I Timothy 2:1–4).** Further, we are to uphold its Constitution and the rule of law as foundational to the freedoms enjoyed by its people. As a ready reference, get a pocket-size copy of the Constitution and keep it handy or put it on your cell phone. Refer to it as often as needed when questions about our Republic arise.[2]

For the Church to be involved in our Republic, we must understand its biblical role and legal relationship to our Republic. The Founding Fathers understood that the Church [religion] must be independent of the government if our Republic was to be distinct from a monarchy. Therefore, to avoid the entanglements of Church and State, as so often occurred in their former countries of Europe, the Framers of the Constitution, in writing the Bill of Rights, gave religion (i.e., the Church) its freedom and independence from legal interference by the government. Our Constitution is specific that the Church in our Republic would remain *distinct* from the government:

Congress shall make no law respecting an establishment of religion, or prohibiting the free exercise thereof; or abridging the freedom of speech, or of the press; or the right of the people peaceably to assemble, and to petition the Government for a redress of grievances. (Amendment 1, the Constitution of the United States of America)

Later, President Thomas Jefferson further clarified what is understood by "distinct." He suggested that *a wall of separation* exists between the Church and the State. Nevertheless, many godly men became elected leaders and officials within the halls of government. Often their Christian values were apparent in making legislation and policies, but without representing or promoting any religious affiliation—something the Framers intentionally sought to protect against.

Therefore, to avoid an "unholy alliance" the Church must remain distinct in purpose and function from government. The Church must be diligent not to become an institution of government, nor should it be nationalistic in its influence **(Mark 12:17)**. (See Appendix: *What is Christian Nationalism?*)

Your Thoughts:

_____

_____

_____

_____

_____

_____

_____

_____

A Warning

Sin and separation from God severely divide our Nation. Only a cataclysmic event can possibly heal the severity of our division. However, this is not the first time we have experienced such division. The 1920s and 1930s saw a divided and tested Nation. Our democratic form of government and the Republic itself descended into social warfare on the streets of our cities as the inroads of the *Ku Klux Klan,* Communism, and Nazism threatened our Republic. World War II brought most of us together again. A biblical truth cited by Abraham Lincoln during another divisive moment in our history—The Civil War—made the point clear.

President Lincoln said, *"A house divided against itself cannot stand. I believe this government cannot endure, permanently, half slave and half free."*

These words were first said by Jesus,

If a kingdom is divided against itself, that kingdom cannot stand. And if a house is divided against itself, that house will not be able to stand. **(Mark 3:24–25)**

Clearly, as a Republic, we cannot endure a divided nation. Our only hope is for followers of Jesus to pray. Pray and seek *aggressively* the welfare of the "city" **(Jeremiah 29:7)**. This is not praying for the success of a favorite political party, but it is asking God to give an infusion of divine wisdom to *all* our leaders—both political and social.

It is praying that God will hear the cries of injustice, hopelessness, and helplessness. And, if he calls upon us to engage directly in meeting the needs of the poor and vulnerable, our response should be like that of Isaiah: *"Lord, here am I! Send me!"* In addition to calling people to faith in Christ and becoming part of His Kingdom, the durability and *unity* of our Republic and our democratic government are to be "job one" in promoting the welfare of the "city."

We must be keenly aware and astute, knowing that at any point, our Republic can face the same fate as the Republic of Rome faced 2500 years ago. There is no guarantee that it will endure. *It may not.* After all, our Republic is still an experiment, *"If you can keep it!"* What do we want to leave to our children and grandchildren? Just another uncertain political party to rally behind, or an enduring Republic that shines brightly on a hill in the hopeless darkness of our age?

Challenged by our higher calling, we need to put aside any notion of returning to a way of life that *used to be.* We can't *return to our Egypt*, hoping to make today like it was *then. That kind of hope is an exercise in frustration.* Instead, God moves forward with a clear destiny in view—a destiny beyond the kings and kingdoms of this world. A destiny we share with Him! But, unhappily, some people are convinced otherwise.

Your Thoughts:

Come Christian Triune God that lives;
Here am I!
Shake the world again.
—Francis Shaeffer

A Closing Thought

A discerning study of the Gospels reveals a different Kingdom than the one many of today's evangelicals are politically seeking. First, Jesus sets before those who would be His followers the manifesto for His Kingdom, *"If anyone would come after me, let him deny himself and take up his cross daily and follow me" **(Luke 9:23)***. Jesus further develops his agenda for the Kingdom of God in **Luke 4:18–19**. And, again in **Matthew 28:19–20**, *"make disciples of all nations (Gk: ethnos–peoples), baptizing . . . teaching them to observe all that I have commanded you."* It is a Kingdom that welcomes all of humanity who believe, as declared in **John 3:16**. The Church finally arrives at **Revelation 7:9–10,** where the culmination of what Jesus intends for His Bride on earth comes into view. Here, a people for His Name gathered from *". . . every nation, from all tribes and peoples and languages . . ."* begin an eternity of collective and exalted praise to Christ.

This Kingdom is very Christ-focused and Christ-consuming. The Church, the expression of God's Kingdom on earth and for eternity, cannot be associated with this world's way of doing things, nor with this world's thinking or philosophy. Reading the Gospels, we see that what Jesus taught is out of sync with the ways of this world—whether it is loving your enemy, forgiveness, managing wealth, caring for the poor, and so on. To what end? *". . [God] who desires all people to be saved and come to a knowledge of the truth" **(I Timothy 1:2–4)**.*

Growing ethnic tensions exist in our Nation today. But, they always have existed, as they do in other nations. Such tensions separate and divide us behind walls of hostility, anger, and hate that often lead to violence. However, for the followers of Jesus, there are different marching orders—the truth of the Gospel of God's Kingdom:

But now in Christ Jesus you who once were far off have been brought near by the blood of Christ. For he himself is our peace, who has made us both one and has broken down in his flesh the dividing wall of hostility by abolishing the law of commandments expressed in ordinances, that he might create in himself one new man in place of the two, so making peace, and might reconcile us both to God in one body through the cross, thereby killing the hostility. **(Ephesians 2:13–16)**

As commanded, we are to move forward to advance the Kingdom of God and bring the lost back home to the Father's House **(Matthew 28:19–20; Luke 15:1–24)**. We pray and seek the welfare of our fellow citizens of this Republic by whatever means the Lord gives us and however the Spirit will use our gifts and talents. When we begin to seek the welfare of *all* people, the Lord's Name is honored, and He is glorified.

As long as we are where we are, we have dual citizenship—the Kingdom of God and our Republic. These are not in conflict—*Seek first the Kingdom of God and His righteousness and all these things will be added to you* **(Matthew 6:33)**.

As His image-bearers we bring the salt and light of God's presence daily into this world of darkness. First to our family, then to our neighbors, then to those at work, our community, and beyond **(I Timothy 2:1–4).** Yes, there will be challenges and problems. Yet with the problems is an abundance of opportunities—hurting people all around us needing encouragement, healing, and God's love. *Each of us is a missionary for Jesus, a sent-one on a mission, and most of the time, it's right where we are!*

As it was with the early Church, so it is with us today. If Jesus is Lord, then Caesar is not—*nor is any other political ruler since or that will ever be.* If Jesus is Lord, no other authority is absolute. Only Jesus Christ and the Kingdom of God are the Christian's first loyalty above all others. *"Thy kingdom come, thy will be done, on earth, as it is in heaven."* Our faith is personal but never private, meant not only for heaven someday *but for here and now.* Go then into your city and show and speak the power of God's love. *Jesus is Lord! And He is Lord of all!*

Your Thoughts:

_____

_____

_____

_____

_____

Let's Talk About It
(Group Discussion for Chapter 5)

1. **Our Roman Connection. (Pages 93–95)** Describe the weaknesses and failures of the Roman Republic? How are they similar (or different) to our Republic?

2. **Forming a Democracy. (Pages 96–99)** Why was there uncertainty about the durability of our Republic? How are those concerns relevant today? Describe the difference between a Republic and a Democracy? Is an Autocracy within a Democracy possible? How?

3. **Our Country and God's Kingdom (Pages 100–103) (1)** Describe the point of tension or balance between obeying the government and God's Kingdom? How do the words of Jesus in **Matthew 22:21** as it relates to you and your dual citizenship? **(2)** As to **"Salt and Light,"** how should you view the outcasts, the vulnerable, and aliens in your society? Are the following verses from the Old Testament relevant today: **Leviticus 19:33–34; Numbers 15:15–16; and Deuteronomy 24:17–22.**

4. **Our Role and Our Nation. (Pages 103–104)** Give some examples of how the idea of the separation of church and state has not always worked in matters of social concern. Why is this?

5. **A Warning (Pages 105–107)** Our Nation is divided socially and politically. As a follower of Jesus, what two things can you do to bridge that fault line?

6. **A Closing Thought. (Pages 108–110)** Describe the difference between Christian Nationalism and the Kingdom of God? (See Appendix)

Additional Notes:

For each of us the time is surely coming
When we shall have nothing but God.
—A.W. Tozer

Chapter 6

What God Says About This World and You

God has a lot to say in His Word about this world and you. The Bible leaves very little to the imagination about what has happened throughout human history. The same is happening today and will occur in the future. He's quite specific!

What God Says About This World

The first two chapters of Genesis tell how God spoke the heavens and the earth into existence along with created beings—*eventually, you and me.* After a short introduction to what God did perfectly, what followed was catastrophic, profoundly undoing God's perfect creation. Chapter 3 reveals the core of what was to be a perpetual human problem—**sin**. Sin defaced the perfect nature and character of humanity as those created in the image of God. However, the effect of sin went beyond the one who bore His image to affect and hopelessly marred the entire created order. **(Romans 8:20–23; 2 Peter 3:11–13)**.

The result of sin infected our fallen race with lying, deception, suffering, pain, miseries, violence, murder, and eventually death.

Sin also brought corruption, wickedness, and idolatry. The early chapters of Genesis reveal the beginnings of sin's lethal toll on humanity. What continues throughout the Bible and throughout human history only amplifies what began when the *fruit of the tree* became more desirable than God. Sin still plagues our world today and will continue to do so until Jesus returns.

In our world today, nations war against nations. Countless numbers of people suffer violence, being held captive by social and political bondage and, at times, even exterminated by nefarious and narcissistic leaders. Sinful behavior of pride, anger, and jealousy began with Cain, the son of Adam and Eve, when he killed his brother, Abel. This senseless murder was the first recorded human death. Since this first act of violence, the world has concluded that killing one another is the final solution to any annoying problem. Daily, the news media chronicles this continuing and seemingly increasing sinful behavior **(Genesis 4:4–8).**

In addition to sin's direct assault on humanity, the collateral damage of sin persistently produces sickness, social injustice, poverty, and homelessness. As we have noted previously, these conditions are pervasive throughout the world. Universal human misery exists because the world is hopelessly immersed and motivated by greed, pride, and corruption. What is the root cause? Sin! This universal condition is Satan's perfect storm as he seeks to destroy and defame God's character by countless accusations of what a poor job He is doing as Creator.

Even "good" nations sometimes do bad things—including ours. For example, we enslaved black people even before we were a Nation. We took land from native Americans through broken treaties, destroying their culture and decimating their population. Furthermore, we continue to victimize Asians and other people of color—the list of social injustices goes on. *But God is a God of justice and righteousness. He remembers!*

Your Thoughts:

_____

_____

What's Up Ahead?

God's Word has a lot to say about what is ahead for this world. One day Jesus gathered His disciples on the Mount of Olives. There He told them what to expect in the future.

"First," He said, "expect to see people being captivated by *false* 'truth-bearers' who will attract many to their message of deception, all packaged as truth. They will promote themselves as those who can be trusted leaders and saviors. These false truth-bearers will promise to satisfy the people's needs and give them a quality of life with everything they want." To make His point, Jesus issues this warning, *"Be careful! Don't be misled!"*

Furthermore, Jesus says, "You will see wars and hear of rumors of wars, all increasing with greater intensity. As it is today, you will see nations going to war against nations and kingdom against kingdom. People will be unsettled. *But don't panic!* All this is part of God's plan. There will be increased famines, pestilence, and natural disasters with more to come. These are all indicators that the end of all things is coming soon. *Get ready!*

"Yes, you, as God's people, will be caught up in the swirl of evil that will abound during these final days. Sin will be rampant everywhere. Because you are my followers, you will not fit the culture of this world. You will be hated, arrested, persecuted, and killed. Furthermore, during these final days, the love of God by many will grow cold, and many will turn away from Me. They will betray and hate each other. Deception will be everywhere. *Be faithful to the end!*" **(Matthew 24:3–14; the free verse is mine)**

The end times described in graphic and cataclysmic terms assure that a final judgment is certain. No one can escape the severity of God's wrath against rebellious and unrepentant sinners **(Matthew 24:1–31; 2 Peter 3:10–13; Read Revelation 16)**.

Your Thoughts:

By Grace You Are Saved

From the beginning, in the Garden of Eden, God's grace and mercy overflowed toward mankind. God stepped forward in grace by killing an animal to make garments of skin for Adam and Eve. *And God clothed them,* symbolically covering their sin **(Genesis 3:21)**. Throughout Old Testament Scripture, God provided forgiveness for sin by daily animal sacrifices. Finally, Jesus, as the Lamb of God, steps forward to sacrifice Himself to take away the sin of the world, once and for all **(Romans 6:10; Revelation 5:8–10)**.

But as people sinned more and more, God's wonderful grace became more abundant. So just as sin ruled over all people and brought them to death, now God's wonderful grace rules instead, giving us right standing with God and resulting in eternal life through Jesus Christ our Lord. **(Romans 5:20–21 NLT)**

One of the greatest experiences of life is to know the joy and peace that comes when you step across the line—the line from where you are in your sin to where God wants you to be—His child, forever free from sin.

Take this opportunity right here to stop reading and acknowledge that, like Adam and Eve, you are a sinner before God and that you need forgiveness. God wants to give you this opportunity to show His grace and mercy to you.

Adam and Eve tried to hide from God. They couldn't, and neither can you. In **1 John 3:20,** God assures you that He knows everything about you. He knows your heart is not what it should be—and even what it could be. The Spirit of Truth speaks to you with no uncertain words in **1 John 1:9**, *"If you confess your sins, God is faithful and just to forgive your sins and to cleanse you from all that isn't right about your life."* Stepping across that line, believe what God says, and receive Jesus Christ as your new life. He alone can take away your sins. He alone assures you of a quality of life called eternal life. Thus, a new home with the Father is guaranteed. Being on God's side of the line, *your sins are forgiven, forgotten, forever. Amen!*

But no one can take that step for you. People can show you where to look, but you alone must take that step across the line and say, "Lord, here I am. A sinner! I give myself to You. Thank you for saving me and making me a child of the King."

Now it's your turn to pray, confess, and believe—yes, and be thankful and rejoice in your new life. ***It is indeed a wonderful life!***

For God so loved the world, that he gave his only Son, that whoever believes in him should not perish but have eternal life. For God did not send his Son into the world to condemn the world, but in order that the world might be saved through him. ***(John 3:16–17)***

Your Thoughts:

What God Says About You

As a follower of Jesus, you are not an afterthought of God's grace. On the contrary, in sovereign love and kindness, He had you in His heart from the very beginning—*"before the foundation of the world"* **(Ephesians 1:3–10)**.

Yet, while you were still a sinner, apart from God and without hope, Christ died for you. The mystery of God's infinite love and mercy is profound—truly beyond your ability to grasp. One may wonder if eternity is long enough to plumb its depth. Yet, if you have received God's grace of salvation, God Himself tells you, *"Your sins and iniquities I will remember no more." "There is now no condemnation for those in Christ Jesus."* Your sins are forgiven, forgotten, forever. Amen! **(Hebrews 10:17; Romans 8:1)**

Lingering in the despair of past or present sin is to deny what God has done for you in Christ. It is to deny who you are! *What you were without Christ is not what you are in Christ.* You are a new creation, an adopted child of the King of kings and Lord of lords. Seen by God as clothed in the robe of Christ's righteousness, you hold in your heart a special invitation to be at the wedding feast of the Lamb—*as His Bride.* Yes, your name is forever written in the Lamb's Book of Life. **(Isaiah 61:10–11; Revelation 19:6–9)**

Remind yourself daily of who you are in Christ. Dare to see yourself as Christ sees you without blemish or sin, radiant in the splendor of His righteousness and glory. He sees you as the one He created you to be, the one you will be when you arrive on heaven's shores and see Him face to face. What a future is in store for you! In the words of Bart Miller's song, "I can only imagine!"

At this very moment, even as you are reading, know you are accepted in the Beloved One. Civilla Martin, in the lyrics of her hymn, *"Accepted in the Beloved,"* captures where you are now and forever in Christ:

In The Beloved

"In the Beloved" accepted am I,
Risen, ascended, and seated on high;
Saved from all sin thro' His infinite grace,
With the redeemed ones accorded a place.

In the Beloved—how safe my retreat,
In the Beloved accounted complete;
Who can condemn me? In Him I am free,
Savior and Keeper forever is He.

In the Beloved, I went to the tree,
There, in His Person, by faith I may see
Infinite wrath rolling over His head,
Infinite grace, for He died in my stead.

Refrain
In the Beloved, God's marvelous grace
Calls me to dwell in this wonderful place;
God sees my Savior, and then He sees me,
In the Beloved, accepted and free.

Do not let the world around you take away who you truly are before God in Christ, nor convince yourself otherwise. This Truth is your strength as you go forward into the world today.

Your Thoughts:

Some of life's greatest conversations happen
When you are alone with God.

Let's Talk About It
(Group Discussion for Chapter 6)

1. **What God Says About This World. (Pages 113-115)** How do the effects of sin impact today's world? What good things do you see in this world that demonstrates God's mercy? *If your feel comfortable sharing*, discuss how your past sins have affected your life.

2. **What's Up Ahead? (Pages 115-116)** What are the two most important things to remember in Jesus' telling of future events? Why are they important? If you are still on earth when these end-time events begin, what are some things you would do in view of Christ's soon-coming?

3. **By Grace You Are Saved. (Pages 117-118)** Describe your salvation experience. How and when did you realize God's grace saved you? *(Compare Acts 22:6–9 and 2 Timothy 1:5)* What words would you use to share Christ with someone who has yet to *step across the line*?

4. **What God Says About You. (Pages 119-121)** How does being totally accepted by God change your behavior? Have you ever doubted God's total acceptance of you? Explain why?

Chapter 7

Eleven Exercises to Grow Strong

To be strong, you need to exercise!
Exercising is simple. All it takes is the will to do it
and to do it regularly.
Yes, it's hard work!

Here are eleven spiritual exercises you can do daily to help you grow strong in today's world. These exercises are concepts previously discussed in the book. They provide a ready reference to help you build the spiritual muscle needed for today's challenges:

(1) Always embrace who you are: <u>**You are from God!**</u> Each morning, look at yourself in the mirror. As you adjust your appearance to meet the new day, adjust your mind to this fact: *"You are not your own. You are bought with a price."* You uniquely belong to God. He has placed in your life the fullness of Christ, who is the fullness of deity **Colossians 2:9–10.** Your identity and worth as a person come from Him who is in you. Now go out and be **His light and image-bearer** so that those around you can hear and see God through your life. **PRAY!**

(2) Remember: The whole world lies in the power of the Evil One. Daily as you engage your unbelieving world, expect challenges and conflicts—persecution! You live in a fallen world where sin abounds. The words and behavior of unbelieving people are tainted by the Evil One. So then, as you live Jesus before them don't be surprised that the world hates you. In **John 15:18-19,** Jesus tells us that's the way it's going to be for His followers. **Your job is to show forgiveness and love. PRACTICE!**

(3) In a world where opponents are vilified and crucified, you are to love your persecutors—your enemies, those who act against you and may actively seek your harm. Jesus tells us how to do this: **Luke 6:27–36.** If you find yourself in a death-threatening situation where your enemy is ready to lop off your head, ask for a couple of minutes to pray for them and their family. Do this to show how much God loves them. **LOVE YOUR ENEMIES!**

(4) Declutter your mind. Get rid of things in your life and mind that are filled with unimportant, useless, and negative stuff. These are things and thoughts that do not contribute to your faith-walk with Jesus. **Nurture eternal things—people!** Our minds can become like overstuffed garages filled with busy, useless, and forgotten *stuff* that takes up precious space. **Intentionally make time *to spend time in the quiet presence of Christ,* listening to Him as He speaks to you.** He will show you how to free up needed space in your mind to make more room for Him **(Revelation 3:20). BEGIN!**

(5) Learn to *enjoy* an intimate relationship with Jesus. He waits to be wanted—by you! With passion, seek to know Jesus through His Word and prayer. Look to see what Jesus would do in various situations of life. Be like Him. **Look for Him** in your reading of Scripture **(Luke 24:27, 45). Stay with it!** After all, you're going to spend all eternity with Jesus. Now is as good a time as any to get to know Him better. *"Turn your eyes upon Jesus, Look full in His wonderful face. And the things of earth will grow strangely dim, In the light of His glory and grace."* **LEARN!**

(6) Be diligent in investigating information. We are drowning in a world of educated ignorance and blindness, often called information. **Be very discerning. We don't need to know everything—only that which helps us be more Christ-like.** Determine the **character** and **performance** of the one who speaks. Character combined with performance are God's standards for anyone who would be a teller of Truth. **(Deuteronomy 18:20–22) Don't rely on one source of information.** A single source of information can become an echo chamber **where lies can be quickly spread. Instead,** *"Cast your bread upon many waters"* **(Ecclesiastes 11:1). Make sure** what you accept as being true is from credible sources *(more than just one),* and then allow it to incubate before the presence of God in prayer and His Word. If we ask, the **Spirit of Truth** will come to our rescue! **(James 1:5) DISCERN!**

(7) Make friends with the Holy Spirit, the Spirit of Truth living in you. Jesus says that the **Spirit of Truth** will guide you into **all truth** that He (Jesus) may be glorified **(John 16:12–15).** Learn to depend on your Helper, the One that Jesus left behind for such a time as this. You need the Spirit's wisdom to filter what you hear and see from the world around you. That includes your TV and other electronic devices. Don't compromise what belongs to God alone. Desperate days require divine discernment. **BEFRIEND THE SPIRIT OF TRUTH!**

(8) Don't politicize your faith or your relationship with Christ. Jesus was not partisan, nor did He engage in the political debates of this world. He had a singular focus—**the Kingdom of God. That needs to be your focus as well.** It's great to be patriotic **but do not attempt to establish God's Kingdom as a national or political entity. He has a different plan—** *His Kingdom come.* **Don't forget** to what Kingdom you belong. **Jealously guard your loyalty to Jesus.** He tells us we can only serve one master—God—not worldly power, influence, or wealth **(Luke 16:13; Luke 9:23).** You belong to Him completely, and He wants you to **behave like one of His own. No divided loyalties!** *"You shall love the Lord your God with all your heart and with all your soul and with all your mind"* **(Matthew 22:37). STAY LOYAL TO JESUS!**

(9) Learn to stay calm. Regardless of what may happen in your world—politically, socially, or from natural or human-caused disasters—remember, "you are from God." God, as Sovereign, is never surprised, nor does He wring His hands when things come unglued. **Neither should you.** Jesus has given you His peace **(His Shalom—*tranquility when surrounded by calamity*) (John 14:27; John 16:33).** This kind of peace is **your convincing witness** to the people around you of what God is like. *"God is our refuge and strength, always ready to help in times of trouble. So, we will not fear when earthquakes come and the mountains crumble into the sea. Let the oceans roar and foam. Let the mountains*

tremble as the waters surge! . . . " **(Psalm 46:1–7 NLT)**
REMEMBER HIS SHALOM! DO NOT FEAR!

(10) Dignify people regardless of social class or color of skin as those who bear the created image of God. **(Genesis 1:27).** Learn to look beyond appearance to see **the imprint of the Creator's touch**. Do not bemoan the reality that your pagan non-Christian neighbors behave like pagan non-Christians. Love your neighbor as God-sent ambassadors in an ideologically foreign land living in a post-Christian society. They cannot help acting as they do. They are in hopeless darkness under the captivity of the Evil One. Every day, *"Clothe yourselves with the Lord Jesus Christ"* **(1 Samuel 16:7; 1 Peter 2:12)**. **REMEMBER, JESUS SAVES!**

(11) Finally, always be thankful to God for everything because all things do indeed work together for His purpose Romans 8:28. And, rejoice! Learn to put a song of joy and praise to the Lord in your heart and upon your lips. *"Always be joyful. Never stop praying. Be thankful in all circumstances, for this is God's will for you who belong to Christ Jesus"* **(I Thessalonians 5:16; Psalm 63:2-5). DO GOD'S WILL—BE JOYFUL! BE THANKFUL!**

No discipline is enjoyable while it is happening—it's painful! But afterward there will be a peaceful harvest of right living for those who are trained in this way. So take a new grip with your tired hands and strengthen your weak knees. Mark out a straight path for your feet so that those who are weak and lame will not fall but become strong. (Hebrews 12:11–13 NLT)

PS: Be sure to give God credit for your newly found strength. Glorify Him!

Your Thoughts:

God delights to keep our faith in tension by trials
To keep our hearts dependent by trusting Him

Let's Talk About It
(Group Discussion for Chapter 7)

1. Which exercises are new to you—something you had never thought about doing? Describe how doing them might help you in strengthening your faith.

2. Select **two or three exercises** to begin your training. Why are they important to you? Explain how you will implement these exercises into your life. Describe how you will measure your progress? **(1 Timothy 4:7–10)**

3. If you could only choose **one exercise**, which one would you say is most important to you? Why?

4. Going to a gym to exercise is sometimes helpful. There you can find someone to help you stay on track. Get with a partner. Describe how having an accountability partner would work for you in doing your exercises? Do you have someone in mind that might be willing to hold you accountable?

Additional Notes:

Disappointment is God's way of dimming the glamour
Of the world and deepening our ability to enjoy Him.

Chapter 8

Conclusion - So What?

Several years ago, I attended a church with an outgoing charismatic pastor. His sermons were compelling. After most sermons, he would regularly say, *"So what?"* Such an expression was his way of saying to the congregation, "Okay, now that you have heard from God's Word this morning, what are you going to do about it?" i.e., *"So what?"*

Like my pastor, I believe that God's Word, salted throughout this study guide, brings you to a *"so what"* conclusion that requires action. His Word brings you this question: "So, what are you going to do with what you have read?"

James 1:22–25 spells it out clearly. *"Be doers of the word, and not hearers only, deceiving yourselves."* These verses describe how the doers and the hearers of the Word behave differently. So you need to determine which group you belong to—the doers or hearers only?

As a follower of Jesus, the study guided you through some of the issues you face in your world. In **Chapter 2**, you saw how easy it is for followers of Jesus to become victims to subtle forms of idolatry and how you can rid yourselves of them. You saw in

Chapter 3 how the Truth suffers in a society where the Lie fits comfortably in the daily discourse of life. Yet, you also saw how important it is for the followers of Jesus to speak the Truth and live it, even at personal cost to you. The wonders of an awesome and loving sovereign God captured your attention in **Chapter 4**—how the immensity of God *intimately* occupies the smallness of your heart. "Christ in you, the hope of glory!" **(Colossians 1:27)** Amazing!

Chapter 5 lays out a mini-civics lesson to help you better understand your Nation. Further, you saw your role as followers of Jesus in the political and social spheres of this fallen world. What God says about this world and what He says about you is in **Chapter 6**. Finally, you engaged in eleven spiritual exercises in **Chapter 7**, taking the principles and insights gained from the previous Chapters and putting them into practice. Finally, this leaves you with the question in **Chapter 8**, **"So what?"** What are you going to do with what you now know?

Will you view yourself differently now that God's Word has exposed vital issues in your life? Will you see the world around you with different and more discerning eyes—seeing the world as God sees it? Are you now ready to pick up your cross *daily*, denying yourself, and follow Jesus—*to grow strong in today's world? The choice is yours.*

Your Thoughts:

The philosopher says there is no death unless there is life.
Jesus says there is no life unless there is death.

Let's Talk About It
(Group Discussion for Chapter 8)
A Review

1. What new thoughts did you discover about God from this study? Explain how you *now* understand them? How will they change your thinking and behavior?

2. What misunderstandings, if any, did you have about God's Word that were clarified by this study? What difference will that make in your faith-walk with Jesus?

3. Would you say that sometimes "you live the lie?" If you care to share, how did "living the lie" affect you and others?

4. What attributes of God did you have the most difficulty accepting and understanding? Discuss some of your hesitations. Be candid with your response!

5. Discuss your thoughts on the affairs of our Nation and the Sovereignty of God. How are these two entities reconciled? Give some examples.

6. What was your big "aha moment" during this study? What are you going to do with it? "So what?"

Jesus, I My Cross Have Taken

Jesus, I my cross have taken,
all to leave and follow you
destitute, despised, forsaken
you on earth once suffered, too.
Perish ev'ry fond ambition,
all I've ever hoped or known;
yet how rich is my condition,
God and heav'n are still my own!

Let the world despise and leave me;
they have left my Savior, too.
Human hearts and looks deceive me;
you are not, like them, untrue.
And, since you have smiled upon me,
God of wisdom, love, and might,
foes may hate and friends may shun me;
show your face, and all is bright.

Go, then, earthly fame and treasure!
Come, disaster, scorn, and pain!
In your service pain is pleasure,
with your favor loss is gain.
I have called you Abba, Father;
you my all in all shall be.
Storms may howl, and clouds may gather,
all must work for good to me.

Haste, my soul, from grace to glory,
armed by faith and winged by prayer;
all but heav'n is transitory,
God's own hand shall guide you there.
Soon shall end this earthly story,
swift shall pass the pilgrim days,
hope soon change to heav'nly glory,
faith to sight and prayer to praise.

Author: Henry Frands Lyte (1825)
Public Domain

Ephesians 6:11–12
Put On All Of God's Armor

Put on all of God's armor so that you will be able to stand firm against all strategies of the devil.

For we are not fighting against flesh-and-blood enemies, but against evil rulers and authorities of the unseen world, against mighty powers in this dark world, and against evil spirits in the heavenly places.

Therefore, put on every piece of God's armor so you will be able to resist the enemy in the time of evil. Then after the battle you will still be standing firm.

Stand your ground, putting on the belt of truth and the body armor of God's righteousness. For shoes, put on the peace that comes from the Good News so that you will be fully prepared.

In addition to all of these, hold up the shield of faith to stop the fiery arrows of the devil.

Put on salvation as your helmet, and take the sword of the Spirit, which is the word of God.

Pray in the Spirit at all times and on every occasion. Stay alert and be persistent in your prayers for all believers everywhere.   (New Living Translation)

The Appendix

To Help Us Pray

When the glory of the Father
Is the goal of every prayer;
When before the throne in heaven
Our High Priest presents it there;
When the Spirit prompts the asking,
When the waiting heart believes,
Then we know of each petition
Everyone who asks receives.

— Author Unknown

What is Christian Nationalism?

Based on an article by Paul D. Miller
With Contributions by Philip Gorski and Samuel Perry

In this abbreviated article, Paul Miller forms his thesis about Christian Nationalism around seven questions that cover the concerns of most readers. Philip Gorski and Samuel Perry also contribute their observations.

What is patriotism, and is it good?

Paul Miller begins with a definition for patriotism, "Patriotism is the love of country. It is different from nationalism, which is an argument about *how to define* our country. Christians should recognize that patriotism is good because all of God's creation is good, and patriotism helps us appreciate our particular place in it. Our affection and loyalty to a specific part of God's creation helps us do the good work of cultivating and improving the part we happen to live in. As Christians, we can and should love the United States—which also means working to improve our country by holding it up for critique and working for justice when it errs."

What is nationalism?

Miller continues by defining what is meant by nationalism. Quoting various scholars, he says, "Nationalists believe that nations are made up of distinctive groups (tribes) that should each have their own governments; that those governments should promote and protect a nation's cultural identity; and that sovereign national groups provide meaning and purpose for human beings."

What is Christian nationalism?

Based on Miller's research, Christian nationalism is the belief that Christianity defines the American Nation. Therefore, the government should take active steps to promote Christian values, even to enshrine officially our Nation as a "Christian Nation." Nationalists believe that America not only has a Christian (Anglo-Protestant) heritage but must assert that it remains a "Christian Nation." Furthermore, research shows that Christian nationalism is a conservative populous movement that promotes anticultural pluralism. This movement has become more powerful and extreme as most of the Nation's population becomes neither white nor Christian (Anglo-Protestant). The *Great Replacement Theory* quantifies this concern for many in the extreme white-conservative Christian community.

What is the problem with Christian nationalism?

As Miller shows, white Christian nationalism evolves into a "us" and "them" understanding of our Nation, thus determining who is and who is not an essential part of the Nation. It uses Christian values, the Bible, and symbols (the Cross) to promote its agenda. "Jesus is white. He is one of us and calls us to defend our Nation," so say the Christian nationalists. In their book, *The Flag and The Cross*, Philip Gorski and Samuel Perry emphasize the movement's motivating force: "Christian nationalism is focused on power, not piety. The Nation should be ruled by Christians (men)."

Further, in the view of Christian nationalists, the government and mainline media have been corrupted by liberal elites that seek national control through social regulations and brainwashing (fake news). Further, by this liberal control, they favor minorities by increasing the immigration population as a block of illegal voters that work against them.

Christian nationalists also believe they are targets of persecution. According to them, this must stop, by "righteous" violence if necessary, to return this Nation to its Christian roots. America's (white Christian America) exceptionalism needs to be reinstated, as it was before the Civil Rights movement of the 1960s.

Gorski and Perry point out that as demographics change white Christian nationalists are starting to turn against American democracy and its institutions. Their operating principle is this: Christian nationalists must defend (their) freedom and maintain social (racial) order. Freedom for "us" and authoritarian social order for "them."

Gorski and Perry continue, "Order is understood in a hierarchical way, with white Christian men at the top. Violence is seen as a righteous means of defending freedom and restoring order. This understanding of freedom, order, and violence is at the heart of Christian nationalism to achieve preeminence as a Christian nation once again."

What do Christian nationalists want that is different from normal Christian engagement in politics?

Miller writes, "Christian nationalists want to define America as a Christian nation and they want the government to promote a specific cultural template as the official culture of the country. Some have advocated for an amendment to the Constitution to recognize America's Christian heritage, others to reinstitute prayer in public schools. Some work to enshrine a Christian nationalist interpretation of American history in school curricula, including that America has a special relationship with God or has been 'chosen' by Him to carry out a special mission on earth. Others advocate for immigration restrictions specifically to prevent a change to American religious and ethnic demographics or a change to American culture. Some want to empower the government to take stronger action to circumscribe what is viewed by them as immoral lifestyles.

"Further, they assert Christians are entitled to primacy of place in the public square because they are heirs of the true or essential heritage of American culture, that Christians have a presumptive right to define the meaning of the American experiment because they see themselves as America's architects, first citizens, and guardians."

How is Christian nationalism dangerous to the church?

Miller contends, "Christian nationalism takes the name of Christ for a worldly political agenda, proclaiming that its program is *the* political program for every true believer. That is wrong in principle, no matter what the agenda is, because only the church is authorized to proclaim the name of Jesus and carry His standard into the world."

The Public Religion Research Institute estimates today there are over 13 million evangelical Christians (14 percent of the total evangelical community) who support Christian Nationalism. It has become an idol for many Christians who have fallen victim for a unbiblical understanding of their calling as followers of Jesus and His Kingdom. However, the true Followers of Jesus march to a different drummer:

And he said to all, "If anyone would come after me, let him deny himself and take up his cross daily and follow me. For whoever would save his life will lose it, but whoever loses his life for my sake will save it. For what does it profit a man if he gains the whole world and loses or forfeits himself?" **(Luke 9:23–25)**

Do not love the world or the things in the world. If anyone loves the world, the love of the Father is not in him. For all that is in the world—the desires of the flesh and the desires of the eyes and pride of life—is not from the Father but is from the world. And the world is passing away along with its desires, but whoever does the will of God abides forever. **(1 John 2:15–17)**

For here we have no lasting city, but we seek one that is to come. **(Hebrews 13:14)**

Can Christians be politically engaged without being Christian nationalists?

Miller concludes his thesis by returning to the subject of patriotism and how Christians can and should participate in this grand experiment called the Republic of the United States. "Yes. American Christians in the past were exemplary in helping establish the American experiment, and many Christians worked to end slavery and segregation and other evils. They did so because they believed Christianity required them to work for justice. But they worked to advance Christian principles, *not Christian power or Christian culture*, which is the key distinction between normal Christian political engagement and Christian nationalism. Normal Christian political engagement is humble, loving, and sacrificial; it rejects the idea that Christians are entitled to primacy of place in the public square or that Christians have a presumptive right to continue their historical predominance in American culture. Today, Christians should seek to love their neighbors (friends and enemies) by pursuing justice in the public square, including by working against abortion, promoting religious liberty, fostering racial justice, protecting the rule of law, and honoring constitutional processes."

Paul D. Miller is a professor of the practice of international affairs at Georgetown University and a research fellow with the Ethics and Religious Liberty Commission.

Philip Gorski is a Professor of Sociology and Religious Studies at Yale University.

Samuel Perry (Ph.D., Chicago) is a sociologist of American religion, race, and politics at the University of Oklahoma.

The article first appeared in its entirety in the February 3, 2021, issue of Christianity Today. Used by permission of Christianity Today, Carol Stream, IL 448 60188.

Additional Notes:

The fact that God's plans for us are perfect
Guarantees that rarely will we understand them.
—Burt Brunemeir - Far East Broadcasting

A Deeper Sound

Oh, a deeper sound the note must make,
Of love's sweet song for God alone;
No surface noise can replicate
The Healing Hand upon the soul.

Carefully, Lord, You have wounded me,
That the fragrance of the broken
Be to You an offering — a pleasant thing,
Of love's deeper sound for You alone.

Healing ointment my Great Physician brings,
To correct, instruct, and bless;
To tune the note for the deeper sound,
Of love's sweet song for God alone.

Donald Zoller, 1986

A Personal Reflection

Throughout the book, the reader may have tried to determine from my writing how I view the world in which I live and my relationship to Jesus, i.e., the framework that makes up my thinking and beliefs. Who and what I am is no secret.

Background

I grew up in a racially diverse community of East Los Angeles, California. Among my friends were Latinos, Asians, and Blacks. Rarely were we aware of our differences and enjoyed the company of our distinctions. While in the military, I was exposed more broadly to an ethnically diverse community. Here, I experience the benefit of working with a team of men with mixed racial backgrounds and beliefs.

Subsequently, I was further immersed in the Latin culture. I lived among the people of Panama, Mexico, and Honduras. and thoroughly enjoyed every moment. Further on in life, I was associated with an international Christian broadcast ministry that regularly put me in touch with those in the Arab and Farsi-speaking world.

Although I heard about "prejudice" and I saw it occasionally in others, personally, I had no real-life experience with it. I thought it strange why some people assumed a sense of entitlement and superiority regarding racial differences. My great-grandfather once told me that if people's blood is the same color, we are all part of the same *human race*, regardless of skin color or cultural background.

Spiritual Formation

I came to faith in Christ in 1954 while in the army. From that point on, I soon became involved in Christian-related domestic and international ministries. I was an "evangelical" Christian throughout my 70 years' walk with Christ. Still, I always enjoyed the freedom God gave me to experience the broader fellowship of His people in other lands, cultures, and diverse communities of faith.

In this broad and extended community of faith, my brothers and sisters in Christ always had something to contribute to my spiritual growth. (I hope I was able to contribute to theirs.) There was always something to celebrate. The color of their skin or their cultural distinctions did not matter. "In Christ" were the formative words that were the most decisive for me.

As a Bible teacher and writer, it troubles me to see some elements within the white evangelical community devalue people of color and not accepting cultural differences. I fail to see those distinctions in the words of Jesus **(John 3:16: Revelation 7:9–10)**. I believe that the closer one walks with God, the greater love we have for all people, and the more we become blind to ethnic differences and distinctions. Our eternal home in Heaven is free of these distinctions. They will not exist. They will be a non-issue when we are in the presence of Jesus, singing our hallelujahs as His Bride.

Further, my spiritual formation was grounded in churches committed to strong Bible teaching. In addition to Bible studies, training sessions, and leadership roles, my spiritual growth also came from my involvement with ministry organizations. These included InterVarsity Christian Fellowship, Wycliffe Bible Translators (Mexico), Crown Financial Ministries, Concerts of Prayer International, Raleigh Rescue Mission, and SAT-7 (a multi-lingual Christian media broadcasting ministry to the churches of the Middle East and North Africa).

My Faith in Shoe Leather

I live in a time when my culture can no longer be my formative source for truth—for what is right and wrong. It radically differs from God's Word and can no longer contribute or support my walk with Christ. I find that media no longer can be trusted to plainly speak the truth. By all indications our culture is flawed by sin. Because of this flawed culture, I am careful not to be captivated by its enticements or seek comfort from it **(Romans 12:2; 2 Timothy 2:4)**. So, as intentionally as possible, I look to the *Truth of Scripture* concerning the world in which I live. At this point in my life, I have come to the following understandings:

As far as humanly possible . . .

1. I seek to live life *Coram Deo* (before the face of God). Face to face with Christ my Savior, will be my eternal occupation and discovery. It is not too soon for me to learn what this means. In part, this means living in intimacy with Jesus, putting aside the clutter and busyness of life so as little as possible obscures my view of Him **(Psalm 27:4, 8)**.

2. I seek to bring every wandering and errant thought into submission to God's Word as the Word of Truth. In so doing, I ask that He regularly interrogates my thoughts and words to be measured and purified by Truth. And by that Truth to see the world and myself as God sees me **(Psalm 119:160; John 17:17)**.

3. I seek to pray—to pray more not with the abundance of words but out of the overflow of my heart. To be spontaneous in conversation with the Lord throughout the day. *Tevye,* the dairyman in *The Fiddler on the Roof,* has always been my model for conversational spontaneity in prayer. Prayer is essential for a healthy relationship with Jesus. It's the only way I know to speak with Him! Lord, teach me to pray! **(Luke 11:1; I Thessalonians 5:17–18)**

4. I seek to engage in active fellowship with other believers in Christ. As one gets older and single, as I am, there is a human tendency to draw back away from others to a quieter and calmer solitary life. Although inviting, this seclusion is not mentally or emotionally healthy, nor is it beneficial to the Body of Christ **(Hebrews 10:24–25)**.

5. I seek to share Christ's love and forgiveness with others in the same way He captured my heart in love by His overwhelming presence in my life **(John 3:16)**.

6. I seek and pursue the Kingdom of Heaven where I have my eternal citizenship. Although I recognize and celebrate my temporal citizenship to our Nation, I intentionally stay clear of the fray of partisan politics. Instead, the passion of my heart is for the "welfare of the city" and those who are so often vulnerable victims of social injustice in our culture **(Jeremiah 29:4–7; Matthew 6:33)**.

These six points are foundational to my worldview. They are aspirational, meaning, I haven't yet arrived! But, nevertheless, they are the lens through which I desire to view my world and make decisions about my life. To put them into practice and keep "the wheels on the wagon" going forward is a constant challenge. I am in a constant learning mode. Perfect, I am not! And my tongue is often ahead of my heart. Until it is my turn to be with Jesus, I will keep stumbling while learning to walk in step with Him. At eighty-six (86) years old, I am still a disciple trying to keep up with Jesus. I am thankful I am not alone! **(James 3:2)**

Now to you, my brothers and sisters in Christ, be encouraged no matter how dark the days may be or how uncertain the future appears, we will all make it home to be with Jesus. We have a hope and an eternal destiny to be with Him. Though our scars of a fallen human nature will disappear, His scars remain to remind all creation, including us, of the price He paid to have us home with Him.

In the meantime, thank you for your encouragement, prayers, acts of kindness, and words of critique and correction – all very much needed. You have all contributed so much to my life on this earth. I deeply appreciate and love you all!

God bless each one of you, and thank you again.

Don Zoller
3/25/2022

Oh my God, my King – Allow your servant
To complete the days appointed to him.
With hands full of purpose.
And a heart full of love.
For my Master and Friend
                    Don Zoller

End Notes

For Those Who Need
More Information

Chapter 1 What A Wonderful World–
Not So Much

1. **Page 15. A description of the Summer of Rage of 1967**
(also referred to as the Long Hot Summer 1967)
https://en.wikipedia.org/wiki/Long,hot_summer_of_1967

2. **Page 15. The story of "What a Wonder World"**
https://wordsmusicandstories.wordpress.com/2017/01/11/what-a-wonderful-world-analysis/comment-page-1/

3. **Page 16. Racial violence in the United State since 1660**
https://www.blackpast.org/special-features/racial-%20violence-united-states-1660/

4. **Page 16. Action Against Hunger statistics**
https://www.actionagainsthunger.org/world-hunger-facts-statistics

5. **Page 17. United Nation Report on homelessness.**
https://www.un.org/development/desa/dspd/wp-content/uploads/sites/22/2019/10/Inclusive-Cities-for-All-31Oct2019-v11-1.pdf

6. **Page 17. World Health Organization (WHO) report on Mental Disorders.** *https://www.who.int/news-room/fact-sheets/detail/mental-disorders.*

7. **Page 25. National Institutes of Health (NIH) Report on Drug Addiction.** *https://www.nih.gov/news-events/news-releases/10-percent-us-adults-have-drug-use-disorder-some-point-their-lives*

Chapter 2 Idolatry – Both Then and Now

1. **Page 34. List of Hebrew deities (Idols)**
   https://en.wikipedia.org/wiki/Category:Deities_in_the_Hebre w_Bible

2. **Page 35. Number of Hindu gods (Idols)**
   https://apnews.com/article/24bfb9b360e30268ce87764b6f65 bb72

Chapter 3 What is Truth?

1. **Page 51. Stanford Encyclopedia of Philosophy – Truth Theories** *https://plato.stanford.edu/entries/truth/*

2. **Page 69. Statistics for numbers of Christians addicted to pornography.**
   https://www.missionfrontiers.org/issue/article/15-mind-blowing-statistics-about-pornography-and-the-church

3. **Page 69. Screen Time Statistics**
   https://elitecontentmarketer.com/screen-time-statistics/

4. **Page 69. Cell Phone Addiction**
   https://www.helpguide.org/articles/addictions/smartphone-addiction.htm

Chapter 4 The Sovereignty of God

1. **Page 74. What does the Name Yahweh mean?**
   https://firelifeministries.org/grow-your-relationship-with-god-blog/what-does-yahweh-mean

2. **Page 77. Gene Edwards,** *The Devine Romance* (Tyndale House Publishers; Reissue edition (March 15, 1993) 233 pages. (Purchase from Amazon)

3. **Page 79. The God Particle**
   https://thinkpoint.wordpress.com/2012/07/05/the-god-particle-an-elusive-piece-to-the-cosmic-puzzle-discovered/

Chapter 5 A Republic – If You Can Keep It

1. **Page 94. Assassination of Julius Caesar**
   https://en.wikipedia.org/wiki/Assassination_of_Julius_Caesar

2. **Page 103. National Constitution Center,** The Constitution
   of The United State *www.constitutioncenter.org*

Before God, it is not what I am,
But what I am willing to become that excites Him most.
Zephaniah 3:17

As I Face the Wilderness

Lord, as I face the wilderness Give me strength to
bear the load,
And the patience to endure the places
Where there is no road.

Give me eyes your pillar of fire to see
Amidst my darkest night;
To know each painful thorn and cutting stone
Prepared by You who always do what is right.

For others who journey on this common path,
Give me shoulders their burden to bear,
Who often stumble like myself,
A comforting word and a tear to share.

But most, give me a heart
That hungers and thirsts for you, Lord,
As I face the wilderness,
To be fashioned and molded anew.

—Don Zoller January 1998

A Word of Thanks

Unless your name is Michael Angelo or Leonardo da Vinci, it usually takes more than one person to create a masterpiece, let alone put together a book like this one. So, in deep appreciation of those who helped me stay out of trouble, I want to say thank you:

Connie Moyes – Who did the text editing for the book. Connie is a former public-school teacher, a Sunday School co-leader/teacher, and a very busy mom and grandmother. Yet, she still found time to edit this manuscript, which I sincerely appreciate. In addition, she brings to the editing task her passion for the Word of God and her commitment to Christ.

David Steele – Performed the important task of content editing. His background as a former university professor, school superintendent, and his daily walk with Christ, was a plus to the formation of this book. I deeply respect both him and his family, who have befriended my wife and me for many years, and his long and abiding commitment to the work of Christ's Kingdom.

Jan Brauer – Jan did the necessary final pre-publication review of the manuscript. As a contributing editor of my previous book, *The Master Weaver*, she, with a keen eye and a common-sense perspective, contributed her excellent journalistic skills to this book. In addition, her passion for Jesus Christ and His Church made her the obvious person for the final review.

And, most importantly . . .

Jesus Christ – _the true author of this book._

God's grace is never governed by our gratitude.

Author's Page
Donald Zoller

The following is a list of published and unpublished works written by the author. You may order published books and articles from the information listed below. Unpublished works are available in electronic form by contacting the author at dhzoller@outlook.com.

Published Books and Articles

Learning to Suffer God's Way – Discovering Purpose in Suffering. *Easton, MD: SAT–7, 2012. 34 pages. ISBN: 9781500354831 (Order: amazon.com)*

The Last Shofar!: What the Fall Feasts of the Lord Are Telling the Church. *USA: Xulon Press, 2014. 319 pages. ISBN:* 815 *9781628711080 (Co-Authored by Joseph Lenard) (Order: amazon.com)*

Alzheimer's and Dementia – This Ugly Disease – A Caregiver's Journey into Pain, Anguish and Hope. *USA: CreateSpace, 2016,* 819 *2019(Rev.). 48 pages. ISBN: 9781533176738 (Order: amzon.com)*

Living Life in the 4th Quarter – Leaving a Godly Legacy. *USA: CreateSpace, 2016. 75 pages. ISBN: 9781539087342 (Order: amazon.com)*

The Master Weaver – God's Story of Donald & Beverley Zoller *USA: BookBaby, 2021. 244 pages. ISBN 9781098384173 (Order: bookbaby.com)*

Walking With Jesus – Devotional Stories to Help Us Walk with Jesus. *"I wonder what it was like to have been one of the Twelve who for three years walked the dusty roads of ancient Israel with*

Jesus . . ." Combined in eight two-page stories (parables) using divine imagination, each disciple tells their story of what it was like to walk with Jesus. (Available online at https://tlcms.org/walking-with-jesus/)

The Author's Corner (2020) – Eleven one-page simple tutorials to encourage you to write your own life story for your family. (Available online at https://tlcms.org/don-zollers-authors-corner-writing-series/)

Celebrating Easter (2021) – A two-part essay on celebrating Easter, but not without the Passover. Jesus, our Passover Lamb, fulfilled perfectly every predictive detail we know as Holy Week. (Available online at tlcms.org, March 11 & 18 Newsletter)

Selected Unpublished Works

Available by contacting the author at:
dhzoller@outlook.com

Advent of Hope 2020 (Article)– Four weekly devotionals as seen in the Four Candles of Advent, plus the Christ Candle. Each devotional brings to light some aspect of Joseph and Mary's journey to Bethlehem to fulfill the meaning of Advent.

A Collection of Sayings, Meditations, and Poems (2020) –Things that for years occupied the flyleaf of my Bible, now have a home in an electronic booklet format, organized by theme and suitable to share.

In Defense of Our Republic (2020) – An essay that expresses the author's concern for the future of our Republic, the United States of America, and the call upon the Church to be the Church, the Body of Christ, in a changing society.

Now to him who is able to keep you from stumbling and to present you blameless before the presence of h is glory with great joy, to the only God, our Savior, through Jesus Christ our Lord, be glory, majesty, dominion, and authority, before all time and now and forever. Amen. **Jude 24–25**

Additional Copies of this Book
are Available From:

The Publisher: Bookbaby Bookstore
Bookbaby.com

Amazon: Amazon.com
(Search by Title or Author)